Brand Management:
Creating and Maintaining a Strong Brand

WALTER WYMER

ISBN-13: 978-1-7750550-0-6
ISBN-10: 1775055000

CONTENTS

1 INTRODUCTION TO BRAND MANAGEMENT

After studying this chapter you should:

1. Understand what is meant by marketing.

2. Understand what types of entities can be marketed.

3. Understand that the desired support will vary depending on the type of object/entity that is marketed.

4. Be able to distinguish between marketing strategy and marketing tactics.

5. Understand the purpose and importance of branding.

6. Understand the different types of organizations in a society and their marketing needs.

1.0 What is marketing?

Marketing is a managed plan for attracting and retaining support. Marketing involves the planning and implementation of activities to attract and retain support. For a business, support might refer to customers (individuals or organizations who buy what the business sells). For a nonprofit organization, support might refer to clients, donors, volunteers, members, or patrons. For a government agency, support might refer to compliance or participation with a government program.

- Marketing refers to the development of plans and the implementation of those plans for the purpose of attracting and retaining support to the entity that is marketed.

Marketing strategy refers to the guiding pattern or method through which the various marketing activities are coordinated for the purpose of achieving the marketing-related goals of the organization. Marketing tactics refers to marketing activities such as advertising or special events that are elements of the managed plan (e.g., annual marketing plan). Tactics are activities that are designed to achieve short-term goals.

The managed plan usually includes an annual program of marketing tactics that will be implemented to achieve a set of goals. Marketing tactics are often communication-oriented. The marketing organization communicates with various audiences of interest to achieve various objectives.

Marketing professionals gather information and conduct marketing research in order to direct the development of marketing strategies and tactics. Because the purpose of marketing is to gain the support of individuals and organizations for the organization, and because marketing involves learning about potential supporters, communicating with potential supporters, and developing relationships with supporters; marketing professionals are a vital resource to the organization. Marketing professionals, with their understanding of supporter audiences, are in the best position to recommend improvements to the organization that will be most appreciated by supporters.

Branding provides a means of differentiating one organization from another. This facilitates developing marketing tactics. It provides a focal point, an object that can be presented to potential supporter audiences.

2.0 Importance of branding

Brand is a commonly-used word, but not a well-understood concept. Everyone knows what it means, yet it is difficult to explain. People can recall brands, yet it is difficult to define brand. People can distinguish a strong brand from a weak brand, but they cannot tell you the nature of brand strength.

In managing organizations, branding is important. Consumer marketers use brands, hoping to attract consumers' attention to what they are selling while consumers are continually exposed to marketing communications. Consumer marketers hope they can make their brands popular. If a brand can become a preferred brand, companies have less pressure to lower prices.

Brands are not limited to consumer products, however. Managers of charities and public institutions think of their organizations as brands. A university with a prestigious brand image enjoys student applications that exceed enrolment capacity. A charity with a favorable brand image finds it easier to attract donations and volunteers.

3.0 Brands in context

Although much is written about brands and branding, authors often fail to appreciate their own assumptions. When one reads books on branding, one cannot help but notice that the authors appear to have a large consumer-selling corporation in mind (although never stated this plainly). However, although large multinational corporations are involved in brand management, what is appropriate for their type of organization may be quite inappropriate for other types of organizations. In this book, I specifically think of a large variety of organizations when I discuss brand strategies and tactics. If a concept discussed in a book is valid, then it should apply across a variety of contexts or the authors should explain the valid contexts for the concept.

4.0 Organization types and their brands

There are three organizational sectors in society: commercial, non-profit, and governmental. We will begin by discussing the commercial sector. These organizations exist to increase the wealth of their owners through making profits. Commercial organizations use branding as a means of distinguishing what they are selling from what their competitors are selling. Not all commercial organizations experience meaningful competition, in which case, branding has less importance as a means of achieving profitability. Economists classify competitive markets into monopolies, oligopolies, monopolistic competition, and pure (atomistic) competition. Table 1 presents some of the major characteristics of the different competitive markets.

Monopolies are organizations that face no meaningful competition. If a monopoly sells a good or service that people must have, need, or really want; it can be very profitable without investing in branding and the necessary advertising. An electric utility, for example, would have little need for branding. In cases in which monopolies use brand management, it is usually for public relation purposes rather than reducing competitive pressure.

Oligopolies are organizations that are part of concentrated industries. A concentrated industry is one in which a small number of organizations enjoy a large majority of the total industry sales. The necessity of branding in an oligopoly depends partly on whether or not customers are consumers or other organizations. Microsoft, Google, or American Airlines need to appeal to consumers and, therefore, invest in brand management. Koch Industries, Nippon Steel, and General Dynamics sell to other organizations and invest relatively little in brand management.

Table 1. Types of Competitive Markets for Commercial Organizations

Competitive market	Characteristics
Monopoly	Single seller of the good Ability to set price Competition is restricted
Oligopoly	A small number of large firms account for majority of buying and selling Ability to set price Competitors typically avoid price competition
Monopolistic competition	Product differentiation (price, quality, brand) Many firms Few entry and exit barriers in long run Some degree of market power (ability to increase price without losing all customers)
Pure (atomistic) competition	Large number of buyers & sellers No barriers of entry & exit Perfect information Homogeneous products (the products are perfect substitutes for each other)

Monopolistic competition is a type of competitive market that has many producers selling products that are differentiated from one another (e.g. by branding or quality). Commercial organizations in monopolistic competitive markets are typically the most active branding organizations. Sellers try to establish a brand as a means of distinguishing themselves from competitors. In cases in which customers see little difference between competitors (sellers of eggs, for example), a heavy investment in branding is required to distinguish one seller from another. This greater investment (increased costs) is justified if sellers can price their product at a premium by convincing buyers that their product is preferable (e.g., Egg·land's Best).

In pure or atomistic competitive markets, there are many sellers and many buyers. Buyers see no difference between sellers' goods. Corn farmers sell their crops to intermediaries who mix corn harvests from many farmers. Corn farmers would not benefit by branding unless they could convince their buyers that their corn was superior, allowing them to charge a premium to recover the extra marketing costs and to realize a greater profit. Branding of these types of goods is generally done at the retail level (selling to consumers) in which the retailer is in a monopolistically competitive market (e.g., Green Giant corn giblets).

4.1 Nonprofit organizations

Most nonprofit organizations are quite different from commercial organizations. They are not created as a vehicle for enriching owners. Nonprofit organizations have no owners. Nonprofits exist to fulfill the purpose (the mission) for which they were created. Most nonprofits do not have customers. Some nonprofit organizations have members who pay membership fees (e.g., YWCA) or patrons who purchase tickets for events (e.g., performing arts). In most cases, the people served by nonprofits do not pay the full cost of what they receive from the organizations. Nonprofits often need to attract donations from donors, unpaid work from volunteers, or grants from other organizations (e.g., government, foundations).

Branding and brand management is an important managerial function for nonprofit managers. Nonprofits need to attract members, patrons, donors, volunteers, and so on. They need support from individuals who believe in the important of their mission in order to fulfill their reason for existence.

The brand, in a sense, *is* the nonprofit. A nonprofit organization's brand is the meaning of the organization in the minds of important audiences (i.e., groups or audiences to whom the organization communicates and wishes to attract support). A nonprofit's good reputation is perhaps its

6

most important asset in attracting support. The organization's reputation is part of its brand.

4.2 Government organizations

Governments and their agencies are more similar to nonprofit organizations than to commercial organizations. Although a government has the power of legislation (including taxation), if it is democratic rather than authoritative, it will want to communicate with citizens. Governments and their agencies may want to keep citizens better informed about government activities and services. They may want greater citizen participation in policy issues. The police (a government agency) may want greater citizen involvement in reporting criminal activity. Political leaders may be concerned about public relations and citizen attitudes. Many governments want to increase economic activity, often through tourism, in their regions. All these situations can be framed as brand management issues.

5.0 Other brand entities

Organizations are not the only objects that benefit from an emphasis on brand management. Individuals and ideas can also be branded and managed accordingly. Authors (novelists, poets) and other types of individuals who produce creative work can be thought of as brands to be managed for increased effectiveness. Novelists, actors, musicians, fashion models, athletes, dancers, writers, pundits, politicians, and other celebrities may engage the services of publicists, promoters, and public relations professionals to influence audiences' familiarity of themselves and audience perceptions. These are all brand management activities.

6.0 A brief history of branding

Scientific discoveries through the ages eventually led to the development of electricity, the steam engine, metallurgy, chemical engineering, and mechanical engineering. The factory, a mechanized facility designed for mass production, was developed. The industrial age began for many societies around the mid-1800s. For perhaps the first time, the supply of goods exceeded the demand for goods for many products. Goods were produced in factories and distributed to other locations.

Production became more concentrated as factories replaced craftsmen as producers of goods. A comparatively small number of manufacturers were able to produce large quantities of goods using mass production techniques. The combined oversupply of goods and reduced number of producers (who had greater resources as a result of industrial concentration) provided an incentive for producers to compete for customers. This resulted in the beginning of the advertising age.

There was a need for stores and manufacturers to distinguish themselves from competitors. Thus, the age of branding began based on the need of retailers and consumer products manufacturers to distinguish themselves from competitors to make advertising plausible. Hence, marketing (with an emphasis on brand management and advertising) emerged as a meaningful business function in North America and Western Europe between 1890 and 1920.

Branding and advertising merged because the objective of advertising is to increase consumer preference for the advertised brand. The greatest amount of advertising is sponsored by large corporations. Hence, much of the writing and research on branding tacitly assumes the branding organization is a large corporation (usually a multinational consumer products corporation). Although the tendency of writers to have these large, complex commercial organizations in mind is understandable, it is unfortunate.

Because much of what has been written is based on the needs of a specific type of organization (i.e., large consumer products corporations), this knowledge is often not practical or valid for other types of organizations.

6.1 The modern corporation

As a marketing professor for over 20 years, I have read many books and articles on marketing and branding over the years. The vast majority of this work views the marketing organization as a large, complex corporation. Most authors do not seem to be aware that they have this type of organization (a consumer products manufacturer or a retain chain, for example) in mind when they write about an organization's inter-functional coordination, or marketing intelligence system. There are two flaws with having this perspective. First, the vast majority of organizations (commercial, nonprofit, or government) are not similar to large multinational corporations. Second, authors of marketing books and articles appear to think of corporations as they were managed prior to 1980.

In the later part of the nineteenth century until the end of the Great Depression, western economies experienced regular boom and bust cycles. Primary industries were highly concentrated (few competitors) and the stock market was easily manipulated by owners of monopolies. To prevent future economic depressions, western societies enacted laws to break up monopolies. In the late 1970's political leaders such as Margaret Thatcher and Ronald Regan began to adopt neoliberal economic policies. Beginning in the 1980's, anti-trade law enforcement was curtailed, creating a period of mergers and acquisitions in which many industries began to concentrate into oligopolies. This period of market concentration (greatly reducing competition) was enabled by the growth and deregulation of the financial services sector (which was regulated after the Great Depression because of the great harm it had caused). Hence, we have returned to a period of economic boom and bust cycles that benefit those in control of industries at great cost to many. The re-concentration of industry (less competition) coupled with the great power of the financial sector has influenced the managerial perspective of many corporate executives.

From the perspective of the corporate executive, less competition is reflected in less need to advertise. Less need to advertise is reflected in less emphasis on brand management. The modern corporation has created an executive incentive system that results in lavish compensation when the corporation meets the expectations of the financial services sector. Financial analysts estimate target measures that indicate high performance. These may be stock price targets, financial ratios, or other financial measures. Executives are highly rewarded if these targets are met. Executives may make decisions that puzzle an outsider, but are rational if one understands the incentives influencing corporate executives.

Authors of marketing books and articles who view the corporation as the best example of a marketing organization, succeeding in the competitive battle if it best satisfies the customer, may be exhibiting an anachronistic perspective. The modern corporate executive may be quite disconnected from the customer and quite in-tune with the financial services industry.

I will attempt to avoid putting this bias into this book on brand management. I will try to make the concepts I present be applicable and relevant for a variety of organizations. I will present brand management has a useful marketing strategy that is beneficial for all marketing organizations (whether a small business or a charity).

7.0 Importance of branding

Branding offers a means of distinguishing an organization from similar, or peer organizations. Without branding, marketers can only attract support for their peer class. For example, a blood collection organization can encourage people to donate blood; whereas the Red Cross can encourage people to donate blood to the Red Cross. With branding, marketers can attract support for their specific organization.

- Target audiences are those groups from whom marketers seek support

For the brand to be useful, its existence and meaning must be communicated to audiences of interest to the organization. If no one has heard of Moe's (a fictitious pizza restaurant), they are unlikely to be a customer. Organizations need to communicate with target audiences regularly. When a group of friends want pizza for lunch, do they think of Moe's? Is Moe's one of the pizza restaurants that come to mind? Target audiences must be familiar with the brand.

- Target audiences must be familiar with the brand

For the brand to be useful to the marketing organization, the meaning of the brand must be established in the minds of target audiences. When friends are considering which pizza restaurant to visit, how does Moe's compare with other pizza restaurants? Is Moe's thought to be worse than average, average, or better than average? Does Moe's emphasize a differentiating attribute such as better tasting pizza, fresher ingredients, faster service, lowest price, or best pizza for the price (best value)?

As people become more familiar with a brand, the meaning of the brand (their perceptions of the brand) develops with greater clarity. Audience perceptions of the brand are shaped over time by their experiences with the brand and by information they have received about the brand. An organization can communicate with its important audiences and, therefore, can control some of information audience members receive. However, people may hear about a brand from other sources as well. Examples of other information sources may be friends' comments about the brand, the news media, and so forth.

Personal experiences with the brand are quite important in influencing audience perceptions of the brand. When the friends had lunch at Moe's what did they think? Was the pizza average, but the price exceptionally low (a good deal)? Was the pizza excellent for a reasonable price? Was the pizza a little better than average, but the restaurant staff seemed disinterested in customers? Did the restaurant smell peculiar? Many variables or attributes of the brand influence audience perceptions. Some attributes are more important than others and should receive more care and attention by the marketing organization. Notice also how audience perceptions are formed--by considering the brand on its own and also by comparing the brand with its peers. People learn what to expect from a pizza restaurant by their prior experiences. All restaurants should be clean; is Moe's clean? How does Moe's compare with other pizza restaurants?

Brand management is a way of managing the organization and communicating to audiences about the organization with the perspectives of target audiences in mind. Brand management provides a means of helping managers to focus on variables they can control and are of comparatively greater importance to audiences.

Investing in the brand can result in a leveraging effect as well. If Moe's is successful and becomes a preferred restaurant, the organization may have a greater probability of success if it opens a second restaurant.

In addition to directing managerial focus and adding leverage, brand management is important because it naturally integrates public relations into audience communications. When the Red Cross communicates to audiences why they should donate blood or why they should volunteer for the Red Cross, these communications also give audiences positive impressions of the Red Cross. Audiences' familiarity with the Red Cross improves. Audiences' attitudes toward the Red Cross improves. In addition to seeking support from audiences, the Red Cross's communications enhance public relations, which deals with establishing familiarity and favorable opinions about the Red Cross.

8.0 Long-term approach to marketing

One of the key problems I see in the marketing management of organizations is a fundamental misunderstanding of the link between marketing activities or tactics and the desired marketing outcomes that motivated the implementation of those marketing activities. Simply stated, managers often expect to see marketing outcomes (effects) from marketing activities (causes) in the short-term (at the conclusion of a campaign, for example). The problem is that short-term outcomes are not only influenced by the immediate campaign, but also by the organization's long-term marketing efforts. Thus, a weak long-term marketing effort reduces the effectiveness of short-term marketing tactics.

A main point is that the effectiveness of an organization's marketing activities is influenced by both short-term marketing tactics and long-term marketing tactics. If the long-term marketing program is not well-managed, then individual marketing initiatives will be less effective. For example, in the short term some universities whose government funding is determined by enrolment levels experience funding cuts when enrolment levels decline. A sudden reduction in government funding often motivates the affected university to implement a marketing campaign to increase enrolment. These marketing campaigns often involve increasing public awareness of the university but often fail to increase enrolment.

Compare the struggling university to a prestigious university. The prestigious university, because it *is* prestigious, attracts far more applications than students it can enroll. The prestigious university is able to take the most highly qualified applicants (because its demand exceeds its supply). Having higher-achieving students and graduates supports the university's prestigious image. Becoming a prestigious university is the result of a long-term reputation-building strategy. A virtuous cycle can be created as the result of long-term marketing effectiveness. The prestigious university is insulated from enrolment short-falls and their negative consequences.

Would a marketing professional's effectiveness be different for a prestigious university than it would for an average university? Most marketing professionals would find that achieving objectives is easier for a prestigious institution. It is also interesting to note that prestigious institutions usually devote more resources and take a more systematic approach to brand management. Marketing efforts, then, are affected by the organization's strategic marketing effectiveness over the long term, as well as the efforts of the organization's marketing professionals in the near term.

It is my advice to marketing professionals to be an advocate for effective strategic marketing in their organizations. Not only will improving the organization's strategic marketing efforts improve the organization's effectiveness in attracting resources to fulfill its mission, it will also help the tactical effectiveness of marketing professionals. Experienced managers know (all other things being equal), that it is easier to attract support for an organization if the organization is well-known, has a great reputation, and is viewed as a stand-out leader in its mission area. Achieving this favorable condition is the result of effective strategic marketing (achieved over the long-term). Effective brand management, the topic of this book, is a key component of strategic marketing.

9.0 Organization of book

The organization of this book emphasizes a brand management framework. To achieve the benefits or outcomes of effective brand management, a long-term marketing strategy aimed at building a strong brand is required. Therefore, the book is designed to increase readers' understanding of brand management in general, but of increasing brand strength in particular.

The next chapter will lay the foundation for subsequent chapters. The next chapter will describe important brand concepts and their inter-relationships. Although not as practically useful other chapters, a chapter that lays a strong theoretical footing for brand management is essential for understanding the concepts presented in the book. There is a great deal of confusion when it comes to brand-related terms. Brand terms are often used interchangeably to represent different concepts in managerial discourse, discourse which is often laced with industry jargon. In the academic literature in which an emphasis ought to be placed on precision, the situation is similar.

The remaining chapters of the book will discuss what brand strength is and how to increase it. Readers' understanding of marketing and brand management will deepen. It will become apparent that to achieve success, an organization must use marketing and brand management concepts to influence the thinking, planning, and decision-making of organizational leaders. Effective brand management requires a long-term commitment to continuous improvement.

Key Terms

Marketing   Marketing refers to the development of
                                   plans and the implementation of those plans

for the purpose of attracting and retaining support to the entity that is marketed.

Marketing strategy	Marketing strategy refers to the guiding pattern or method through which the various marketing activities are coordinated for the purpose of achieving the marketing-related goals of the organization.
Marketing tactics	Marketing tactics refers to marketing activities such as advertising or special events that are elements of the managed plan (e.g., annual marketing plan).
Monopolies	Monopolies are organizations that face no meaningful competition.
Monopolistic competition	Monopolistic competition is a type of competitive market that has many producers selling products that are differentiated from one another (e.g. by branding or quality).
Oligopolies	Oligopolies are organizations that are part of concentrated industries. A concentrated industry is one in which a small number of organizations enjoy a large majority of the total industry sales.

Pure or atomistic competition	In pure or atomistic competitive markets, there are many sellers and many buyers. Buyers see no difference between sellers' goods.
Tactics	Tactics are activities that are designed to achieve short-term goals.
Target audiences	Target audiences are those groups from whom marketers seek support

2 BRAND CONCEPTS

After reading this chapter you should:

1. Understand what is meant by marketing orientation.

2. Understand various brand concepts.

3. Understand the importance of desired brand outcomes.

4. Understand that the purpose of brand management is to attain desired marketing outcomes.

5. Understand brand-related outcome concepts.

1.0 The importance of distinguishing various brand concepts

Managers of nonprofit organizations are increasingly adopting a brand management framework when thinking of how to improve their organizational outcomes through communications and public relations activities. It is not uncommon to hear a nonprofit executive or university president refer to the need to build or strengthen their brands.

Interest in the brand and brand-related area has also been attracting greater attention among nonprofit marketing scholars. Nonprofit marketing researchers are examining an array of related topics like brand orientation and brand personality. Unfortunately, there is little consistency between authors on what the various brand terms mean. Many authors fail to define the brand terms the use, wrongly assuming they and readers have a common understanding. One problem is the use of business jargon. For example, managers use the term "brand loyalty" generally to refer to consumer brand preference, customer retention, or donor retention. Unfortunately, brand loyalty has its own meaning, as does brand preference, customer retention, and donor retention. Brand equity is often confused with brand strength.

It is quite important to specify the meaning of various brand concepts and how they relate to each other. The relationships between brand concepts cannot be understood if the concepts are conflated or the same brand terms are carelessly used to refer to different concepts. This sloppy use of brand terms and brand concepts is a problem because managers cannot properly understand cause and effect relationships involved in branding without having a clear understanding of the concepts. Marketing planning cannot be effectively performed until managers have a clear understanding about which brand variables they should emphasize in their planning. Hence, we will provide clarity in this chapter by describing important brand concepts.

2.0 Brand concepts
2.1 Marketing orientation

Recall that the purpose of marketing is to attract support to the organization. What is meant by support? Support refers to the desired response a marketer is seeking from a target audience or group. This might be a vote, a donation, volunteering, signing a petition, a membership, a purchase, and so forth. For a business, this might mean customer patronage or retention. For a nonprofit organization, this support might mean volunteers, donations, grants, or members. For a government agency, support might mean greater citizen participation.

Marketing orientation refers to a mindset, way of thinking, or tendency to predominately view organizational issues from a marketing perspective.

A marketing oriented organization uses marketing thinking (a marketing mindset or perspective) not as a specialized area of the organization but as a general management orientation. Through education and experience, a marketing oriented manager's general direction of thought, inclination, or interest is toward marketing concepts and marketing tactics.

A marketing oriented manager may think more about how the organization is perceived by important target groups than would an accounting oriented manager (as an example) who may be more focused on controlling costs and managing cash flow. A marketing oriented manager might be more motivated to engage in marketing tactics to influence external perceptions of the organization and to attract and retain supporters. This is not to say that a marketing oriented manager will not be concerned with internal operational issues or accounting issues. However, marketing oriented managers would be unlikely to see their primary role limited to internal operational issues.

A marketing oriented manager views the organization's success as dependent upon the organization's ability to attract and retain supporters. Hence, a marketing oriented manager would see communicating with external audiences as a necessity, a priority. The type of managerial orientation prevalent in an organization's leadership influences how problems and their causes are perceived, which influences the choice of solutions to managerial problems.

2.2 Brand

A brief perusal of an English dictionary will make one aware that there are often multiple definitions for a single word. The word *brand* shares this characteristic. When brand is used as a verb, (as in *to brand*) it refers to placing an identity on a target object (organization, place, person, idea, good, service, intellectual property, and so forth).

Brand, when used as a noun, refers to a target group or audience's comprehension of the branded object. Thus, brand refers to a target group or audience's comprehension of a brand object based on information they have received about the branded object and experiences they have had with the branded object.

When managers discuss "their brand," they are usually referring to managing the way in which their target audiences think of or perceive their brand object (product or organization, for example). *Brand image* is a term often used to refer to brand, which is also used to refer to a target audience's comprehension of the meaning of the brand object.

2.3 Brand object

Brand object refers to the entity that is the target of branding (or brand identification). This can be an organization, place, person, idea, social movement, good, service, intellectual property, and so forth.

Exxon-Mobile is the name of a large corporation, but the corporate name also distinguishes its products (gasoline, for example). Hence, Exxon-Mobile represents two brand objects: the corporation and its products. Another corporation, Proctor and Gamble, gives different brand names to different products (Tide and Cheer, for example) and variants of those products (Tide Pods, Tide with Acti-Lift, Tide plus Bleach Alternative, Tide Free, for example).

In the nonprofit sector, the brand object is usually the organization. Well known charities like the United Way, The Salvation Army, and World Vision are strong brands. People recognize the organization's names, their logos, or other symbols (for example, the red Salvation Army donation kettle and the bell ringer during the Christmas season). There are variations, of course. Susan G. Komen for the Cure is a charity (and brand) that supports research and education related to breast cancer. The Susan

G. Komen for the Cure charity has a well-known fundraising event which has also become a brand object (the Susan G. Komen Race for the Cure).

Individuals can also be brand objects. When a famous actor (Tom Cruise) is featured in a new movie or popular author (John Grisham) publishes a new book, the movie and the book are more easily marketed because of the respective brand strength of each person. An artist's work and the artist become jointly associated as a composite brand object. People have an understanding of who Tom Cruise is based on his movies they have seen, what they have read about him in the popular press, and what they heard about him from television gossip shows. Often artists and celebrities hire public relations professionals to promote them as brands and to influence their coverage in the media. Record companies and book publishers market their musicians and authors as brands in order to increase audience interest.

2.4 Brand attributes

Brand attributes refers to the nature, characteristics, or qualities of the branded object. The brand object is comprised of a set of attributes. Some attributes are more noticeable (salient) than others. A target group will consider some attributes more important than others.

A dental practice (a small business providing a professional service) can be thought of as a brand object with brand attributes. Many attributes can serves as components of the brand object. The brand, that gestalt (or comprehension of the brand's meaning) is formed in the audience's mind by differential importance given to various attributes. The brand attributes for a dental practice (the brand object) can be its location, sign, waiting room furnishings, cleanliness, diplomas and licenses framed and hung on walls, and so forth. Other attributes might be patient waiting times, style of discourse between receptionist and patient, and empathy (and other personality traits) of the dentist. Some of these attributes may be unimportant to patients and some might be very important. Marketing professionals need to understand which attributes are most important, need to make sure their brand objects are excellent with respect to those important brand attributes, and then need to communicate their brand object's excellence on those attributes to important audiences.

2.5 Brand orientation

A managerial orientation refers to a mindset, way of thinking, or tendency to predominately view organizational issues from a certain perspective. A brand orientation refers to a type of marketing orientation that emphasizes the achievement of organizational goals through managing the organization's brand.

A marketing orientation implies an emphasis on attracting and retaining supporters. A brand orientation implies an emphasis on attracting and retaining supporters by (1) continuously improving the brand object in ways that are meaningful to important supporter audiences, and (2) by increasing brand strength. A brand orientation requires managers to be highly informed with respect to the organization's external environment. The brand object cannot be improved in ways that are meaningful to supporter groups unless managers are aware of what supporter audiences think about the brand object, about competing brands, and about supporter group preferences. A brand orientation requires an emphasis on communicating with supporter audiences. Effective supporter communication requires an understanding of supporter groups that an internally-focused manager would not acquire.

2.6 Brand management

Brand management refers to the development and implementation of plans pertaining to the brand object. Brand management consists of setting objectives, selecting a strategy, and developing tactical plans to achieve brand-related objectives.

Brand objectives for a pizza restaurant (our business example) might be to increase from the second most preferred brand to the first most preferred brand. A goal refers to desired managerial outcomes. Brand goals and objectives state which brand-related variables or outcomes will be emphasized in the planning period as well as the degree of improvement sought. A charity's goal might be to increase donor retention from 40 percent to 45 percent. A police department (our government agency example) might be to increase citizen approval rating of the police department from 20 percent to 30 percent.

Once the goals or objectives are determined, a brand strategy is selected. The brand strategy reflects an overall direction or general emphasis. The brand strategy refers to the general approach used to achieve the brand goals and objectives. A pizza restaurant's brand strategy may be to emphasize fast delivery (if we fail to deliver your pizza in 30 minutes, you get the pizza free). A charity's brand strategy might emphasize resource stewardship (all your donations go to help those in need, not pay for administrative costs). A police department might emphasize a community policing approach rather than having patrol cars respond reactively to emergency calls to reported crimes.

Brand management tactics or activities refer to the specific activities that will be implemented throughout the year in order to achieve the goals and objectives. Once the goals are set and the strategy choice determined, a year-long plan may be developed that integrates separate components throughout the year. The pizza restaurant may implement periodic promotions and advertising campaigns. The charity might implement various events and communication campaigns directed toward various target audiences. The police department might make guest presentations in schools and at public meetings, and may increase the presence of regularly-assigned police officers to specific areas.

The management of a brand represents the means to an end; that is, managers develop and promote a brand in order to attain desired outcomes. Managers try to influence how target audiences perceive their brands. However, managers have limited control over audience perceptions of the brand object. Mangers can control the nature and attributes of the brand object. They have some control over how the target group is exposed to the branded object. Managers can control aspects of the communications they send to a target group of interest. However, the target group's experiences with the brand object and information about the brand object from other sources will also influence a target group's comprehension of the brand object. Also, the target group's comparison of the brand object with its peers and substitutes influences its comprehension of the brand object.

Therefore, a variety of influences act upon a target group's comprehension of the brand object. A brand object that is perceived to be inferior to those in its peer group will be a weak brand, and, thus, a poor performing brand with respect to its ability to attain desired outcomes.

2.7 Peer brands

Peer brands refer to those other brands audiences consider to be alternatives to a target brand. When supporters think of a brand, their evaluation of the brand is somewhat determined by how the brand being evalu-

ated compares to similar brands. Those comparison brands are the evaluated brand's peer brands. McDonald's (a fast-food, corporate-chain, hamburger restaurant) peer brands might be Wendy's, Rally's, Jack in the Box,
Carl's Jr., Burger King, Hungry Jacks, or Quick. Members of a peer group
are determined by the target audience's perceptions. For example, for resi-
dents of a particular city, peer brands in the local animal welfare charity
class might be the Humane Society, the ASPCA, and a variety of charities
targeting specific animal species (dogs) or specie breeds (greyhounds). Peer
brands for a local municipal (city or town) police department would be
fewer, but might consist of other area municipal police departments, the
county (council) police department, or the state (provincial) police department.

When members of a group are developing their perspectives, perceptions, and opinions of a brand through exposure to information about the
brand and experiences with the brand, they also compare that information
and their experiences with what they know about the brand's peers. Audiences' perceptions of a brand are shaped through a combination assessing
the brand individually and in comparison with peer brands.

2.8 Brand identification

Brand identifiers refer to brand attributes (e.g., name, logo, symbol, or
other distinguishing features) that are used to identify or distinguish a brand
object. Marketing professionals find that branding or identifying their
brand objects with names, logos, symbols, and other distinguishing features
(called brand identifiers), aids in distinguishing the brand object in marketing communications.

Managers can assign different *brand identifiers* to their brand objects to
help distinguish their brand object. A dentist who is not going to invest in
marketing might simply put a sign with "Dentist" on the front door. This

dental practice will be associated with the name of the dentist (Dr. Smith) and is dependent upon location (passersby notice the dental office) and word-of-mouth referrals from patients for new patient acquisitions. Another dental practice may create a brand name (Smile Care) and develop a distinctive logo. Smile Care can use its name and logo in its advertisements, business cards, web site, and other communication pathways.

One charity named itself The Salvation Army, developed a logo, established a differentiated annual campaign that is recognized by having individuals who ring bells, near a red collection kettle, located outside commercial establishments, during the Christmas season. The charity's staff leadership wears distinctive uniforms (with hats) that have a combined Christian and military appearance.

2.9 Brand positioning

Brand positioning refers to an aspect of brand management strategy that pertains to decisions about how managers want their brand perceived by a target group. Positioning planning can include decisions about how managers want their brand perceived by a target group generally, and in comparison to peer (i.e., competing or alternative) brands. Brand positioning can include managerial efforts to rank the target brand against peer brands (nominal rankings such as leader, challenger, follower, or specialist; or ordinal rankings such as first, second, or third).

2.10 Brand promotion

Brand promotion refers to managerial activities to communicate to a target group with respect to the brand. Brand promotion tactics are usually intended to influence a target group's behavioral response indirectly through various communication objectives like increasing brand familiarity, improving brand attitude, and so forth.

2.11 Brand personality

One brand positioning strategy is influencing a target group's comprehension of a brand to include human personality traits. The objective of this strategy is to favorably differentiate a brand from peer brands. Prior research has shown that some brands can be differentiates using personality traits. Marketing scholars working in the nonprofit subfield have given this area recent attention.

In this book, I will not treat brand personality as an important brand management tool. I recognize that it is currently a popular topic. However, the usefulness of brand personality as a brand strategy is quite limited. Generally, brand personality scholars groups brand personality traits into five categories: (1) Openness to new experiences, (2) Conscientiousness, (3) Extraversion, (4) Agreeableness, and (5) Neuroticism.

Imagine that you read a research study that reports a survey in which survey participants were asked to complete a questionnaire that scored a personality trait test on a list of four peer brands (restaurants, for example). The research scholars report finding that the peer brand (restaurant) with the greatest market share is differentiated from the other peer brands by the following personality traits: philosophical, systematic, bold, sympathetic, and relaxed. (These five traits are taken from the categories described in the previous paragraph.)

How would a marketing or brand manager use this information? For simplicity, I will focus on just one trait—relaxed. How does an organization make its brand perceived to be relaxed? How relaxed should an organization try to make its brand? Can the organization have confidence that if it is successful in getting audiences to perceive its brand as relaxed, will this result in favorable outcomes for the organization?

I recommend managers avoid using brand personality as a brand strategy. Some marketing scholars and advertising professionals tend to overestimate the importance of consumer products in the lives of consumers. They believe that consumers can have close relationships with their consumer brands. They believe that consumer brands become a central part of consumer self-images. These beliefs have led to a conviction that brand personality is a linchpin in the consumer brand—consumer identity relationship. Unfortunately, there is little evidence that consumers, in general, have such a strong concern about their product choices. This is little evidence that consumers, in general, have "relationships" with their consumer product brands.

Taking on a brand personality strategy creates a distance between the brand object and its brand attributes and what it communicated to target audiences. If individuals have an interest in a brand object class (milk, for example), they are likely to make their support choice (which brand to purchase in this example) based on a comparison of brand attributes. Most people would choose a brand of milk to purchase based on price and freshness (estimated by expiration date information on milk label). People are unlikely to care that advertisements for a brand of milk claim that the milk brand is relaxed.

In this book, I will advise the reader to make the brand object excellent. Distinguish the brand object on brand attributes that matter to audiences from whom support is sought. Then communicate this superiority to target audiences. The marketing communications about the brand is derived from the actual differentiation of the brand object. This contrasts with the methods of advertising managers portrayed in movies and television shows in which advertising effectiveness is not based on brand object superiority but on the creative imaginations of advertising agency brainstorming session.

Advertising creativity can be quite effective in attracting audience attention to an advertisement. Audience attention to an advertisement and repeated exposure to an advertisement can embed the brand name in the audience memories. This is helpful. However, to communicate human personality traits to a brand object in the advertisements seems to misunderstand the reason an audience would support a brand.

2.12 Brand strength

An organization becomes brand orientated and emphasizes brand management as a means of achieving successful organizational outcomes. The relationship between the various brand management tactics at the organization and successful outcomes derived from a favorable response from target groups (customers, donors, alumni, and so forth) is mediated by brand strength. Theoretically, then, marketing tactics serve as antecedents to brand strength. Brand strength serves as an antecedent to outcome constructs. Therefore, we will now discuss brand strength.

3.0 Desired brand outcomes

As discussed previously, branding provides a means to an end. An organization practices brand management because it believes this will allow it to attract greater support than if brand management were not the guiding management framework. There are various ways to measure support, depending on the nature of the organization and other factors. A business might be interested in total sales, customer brand preference, or customer retention. A nonprofit organization might be interested in average donation size, donation frequency, donor retention, bequest intentions, or donor event attendance.

With respect to outcome variables related to support, the variables are generally either direct or indirect. Often, managers want to assess the effectiveness of the different marketing activities or tactics that comprise the marketing plan. I can be difficult to link an increase in support to a specific marketing activity. A specific charitable fundraising campaign is designed to attract support (donations) during the campaign period. In this case, donations can be linked to the campaign, enabling an assessment of the campaign's effectiveness. The fundraising campaign allows for direct measures of its effectiveness. Total contributions, donor acquisition, average contribution, and so forth, are available as direct outcome measures of fundraising (the marketing tactic) effectiveness. This, the goals of the fundraising campaign can be compared directly with the campaign's outcome measures.

Other marketing tactics cannot be directly linked to outcome variables. A charity may also employ marketing tactics to improve public awareness, familiarity, and attitudes. Obviously, the fundraising campaign will be more effective if the charity is well known and enjoys a favorable reputation. Even though the regular marketing communications are an important component for helping the organization to attract support, it is difficult to determine the effectiveness of the various communication tactics. The influence of the marketing communication tactics on attracting support is indirect. The communication tactics increase brand strength. When marketing tactics designed to directly attract support (fundraising campaign, for example), the increased brand strength makes the direct tactics more effective.

In cases in which a marketing tactic directly influences a desired outcome variable, direct measures are required. In cases in which a marketing tactic indirectly influences a desired outcome variable by first (directly) influencing an intermediary variable (brand strength, for example), a measure of the intermediary variable is needed to assess the effectiveness of the marketing tactic. Following the brand strength example, the effectiveness of the various communication activities can be assessed by measuring their effect on brand strength.

3.0 Indirect brand outcome variables

An indirect brand outcome variable refers to an intermediary variable. A marketing tactic's effect on the desired outcome variable (some support-related variable) is accomplished through the influence of an intermediary (or mediation) variable. Mediation variables have a leveraging effect on the desired outcome (support-related) variables. As the mediation or intermediary variables increase in strength, they influence the effectiveness of marketing activities. I will discuss some of the more important mediation variables next.

3.1 Brand equity

Brand equity refers to an economic valuation placed on the brand. Prior research has presented various ways of estimating brand equity. Brand strength is an antecedent of brand equity. That is, a strong brand influences a greater level of brand equity than if the brand were weaker. The brand equity concept was developed due to financially-oriented managers' desire to derive a monetary outcome measure that could indicate the level of return for the investment in branding activities. Also, if a monetary estimate of the brand could be determined, then that estimate could be considered as an asset that could be used for financial purposes.

3.2 Brand recall

Brand recall refers to a brand's accessibility in a target group's memory. A high level of brand recall implies that the target group is generally able to readily access its memory with respect to the brand. Usually this is measured by some type of recall question that requests that an individual list the first three to five members of the brand object's class (e.g., please name five charities). Consumer behavior researchers have found that consumers will usually have a *consideration set* of three to five easily recalled (similar to top-of-mind awareness) peer brands when making a relevant purchase decision.

3.3 Brand preference

Brand preference refers to a target group's greater liking for a specific brand. For example, a consumer may have a brand preference for *Tide* laundry detergent. Brand preference is a leading (not absolute) indicator for repeat brand support (purchase, donation, vote). A circumstance may arise in which the target group perceives an alternative brand to be a more attractive choice (a competing laundry detergent is on sale, a new laundry detergent is given away as a free sample). The experience with the alternative brand may or may not influence the level of brand preference for the original brand. Researchers are quite interested in repeat brand support from a target group because of its implications for the organization's success. Unfortunately, some prior research has erroneously used the term brand loyalty when actually referring to repeat brand support. Often these types of conceptual errors occur when researchers confuse antecedents with outcomes (caused by insufficient construct or nomological net development).

3.4 Brand loyalty

Brand loyalty refers to the degree to which an individual or group feels devoted (feels a bond to and an allegiance with the branded object) to the branded object. Brand loyalty acts as a moderator in the relationship between the availability of alternatives and target group behavior. The level of brand loyalty reflects a target group's level of bias toward the branded object when making relevant decisions. Note the distinction between brand preference (an attitudinal choice predisposition) and brand loyalty (an emotional state reflecting a need to protect, support, and the willingness to make a personal sacrifice for the branded object). Brand loyalty may be rare with respect to consumer products, but may be more common with political leaders, political parties, activist organizations, or charities (brand objects that have the ability to exemplify and reflect a value and identity concordance between the branded object and the target group).

3.5 Brand strength

Brand strength refers to the degree to which a brand is well-known to a target group, is perceived favorably by a target group, and is perceived to be remarkable by a target group. Hence, we conceptualize brand strength as having three dimensions (see Figure 1): brand familiarity, brand remarkability, and brand attitude. *Brand familiarity* refers to the level of knowledge the target audience has about the branded object. *Brand remarkability* refers to the degree to which a branded object is perceived by a target group to be extraordinary. *Brand attitude* refers to the degree to which a branded object is perceived favorably by a target group.

4.0 Attributes and benefits

From the perspective of a target audience, brands provide a bundle of benefits that satisfy its needs. Hence, it is important to have an understanding of basic attribute and benefit concepts.

4.1 Brand attributes

A brand attribute refers to a quality or feature regarded as a characteristic or inherent part of the brand object. It is helpful to think of a brand attribute as a quality, characteristic, trait, feature, aspect, or property of a brand object.

4.1.1 Types of brand attributes

Brand attributes can either be actual features of a brand object (a car's fuel economy, for example) or imagined features of a brand object (Gucci sunglasses are prestigious). The perceived quality, prestige, or exclusivity of a brand may be derived from imagined attributes. An individual really has no objective means of evaluating these attributes, but believe them to be true. Imagined attributes are often the result of image advertising campaigns.

The popularity of Nike basketball shoes soared as a result of the Michael Jordan endorsement and advertising campaigns. The shoes were the same as before. The actual features of the shoes remained the same. However, the brand's association with Michael Jordan imbued the brand with imagined attributes to meet additional target audience needs.

One way to describe attributes is whether they are real or imagined. Another way of classifying attributes is based on how members of a target audience can evaluate an attribute to determine its ability to delivering benefits. There are three types of these attributes. They are search, experience, and credence attributes.

Search attributes are those attributes that can be evaluated prior to consumption, use, or experience. For example, an individual can easily find the price of a hotel room, an airline schedule, television picture quality, and computer memory.

Experience attributes can only be evaluated after consumption, use, or experience. For example, an individual can really only evaluate the quality of a restaurant dining experience by having that experience.

Credence attributes cannot be evaluated even after consumption, use, or experience. Professional services often contain some credence attributes. Take, for example, a visit to the dentist. An individual cannot really determine the degree to which the dental service was excellent (a tooth repair that lasts 20 or more years) or merely average (the tooth repair will last 15 years) or even below average (the tooth repair will last 10 years). Individuals will rely on other cues as indicators of quality. For example, if a dentist is empathetic to the patient's discomfort, an individual might feel that the dentist is very good.

4.1.2 Relative importance of brand attributes

A target audience will place varying levels of importance on the different brand attributes. It will perceive some attributes to provide benefits that are more important than the benefits provided by other attributes. For example, a given target audience may want a pair of designer sunglasses to feel self-confident and stylish. The prestige associated with a designer brand, like Gucci, might deliver this self-confidence benefit to a target audience. We can say that prestige is an attribute of Gucci sunglasses. We can say that this attribute is important to our example target audience. With respect to our prior attribute classifications, we can say that the prestige attribute is an imaginary attribute. We can also say that it is an experience attribute.

If there is a brand attribute that a target audience perceives to be the key factor in choosing among a set of brands, then we call that determinative attribute a diagnostic attribute.

4.2 Benefits

A benefit refers to a good or helpful result or effect. The helpful or good effect of a brand attribute is manifested in satisfying one or more of the needs of a target audience.

4.2.1 Types of benefits

Like attributes, benefits can either be real or imagined. An example of a real benefit is medicine prescribed by a physician when you are sick. You take the medicine, it cures the disease or reduces the symptoms, and you feel better.

Similarly, one can watch a television commercial about a new herbal remedy that is supposed to improve one's sexual performance. The herbal remedy really has no bioactive influence on one's sexual performance, but, nevertheless, one feels a bit more confident after taking the herbal remedy. Although the benefit is imaginary one feels better because one expects to feel better after taking the herbal remedy. This is known as the placebo response. This is similar to that feeling of self-confidence one gets from wearing a pair of Gucci sunglasses or driving a BMW.

Another way to think about classifying benefits is to categorize a benefit as either a functional benefit or a psychological benefit. Functional benefits are provided by the most basic properties of a brand. Food provides the functional benefit of reducing hunger. Drink provides the functional benefit of quenching thirst. Sunglasses provide the functional benefit of reducing sun glare from our vision.

Psychological benefits satisfy one or more of our psychosocial needs. Those Gucci sunglasses provide a basic functional benefit. But they also provide a psychological benefit by giving member of Gucci's target audience more self-confidence.

4.2.2 Matching benefits to needs

If a brand attribute provides a benefit, it means that the attribute was able to help satisfy a need of a target audience member. Hence, attribute benefits are manifestations of the needs they help to satisfy. This concept, the matching of attributes to benefits, is quite important to brand managers. Strategically, brand managers should make sure that the most important benefits target audience members want to satisfy by *their* brand's attributes better than other brands.

Figure 1 matches benefits with the needs they satisfy. Functional benefits help satisfy utilitarian needs. Psychological benefits help satisfy value expressive, social expressive, or ego enhancement needs.

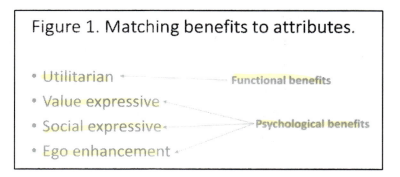

Figure 1. Matching benefits to attributes.

- Utilitarian — Functional benefits
- Value expressive
- Social expressive — Psychological benefits
- Ego enhancement

An important concept to remember is that attributes *only* provide benefits if they help to satisfy one or more of our needs. The type of benefit an attribute provides is determined by the type of need it satisfies. A brand attribute can provide more than one benefit because it may help to satisfy more than one need.

Utilitarian benefits are functional benefits that one experiences from the core (functional) attributes or features of the brand object. For example, a shirt provides the utilitarian benefit of clothing. The shirt covers our body, and helps to protect us from the cold or sun.

Value expressive benefits are a type of psychological benefit that helps to satisfy one or more value expressive needs. Value expressive needs represent a need to express who you are, what you stand for, and your values. For example, an individual may chose a shirt with the Greenpeace logo printed across the chest area. Wearing a shirt with the Greenpeace logo allows members of the target audience to express their environmental values. It allows target audience members to show others a personally important cause.

Social expressive benefits are a type of psychological benefit that helps to satisfy one or more social expressive needs. Social expressive needs helps one to be accepted in one's desired social network, to gain the respect of others, and to be a part of a group that is personally important. The Harley Davidson motorcycle brand appears to satisfy social expressive needs. A visit to the Harley Davidson website reveals a wide array of clothing and accessories individuals can buy to signify the group to which they belong. Many members of Harley Davidson's target audience wear the brand to symbolize their social network.

Ego enhancement benefits are a type of psychological benefit that helps to increase one's self-esteem, helps one to feel better about oneself, and helps one to become the person one wants to be. Many prestige brands provide ego enhancement benefits. Owning a BMW or Mercedes helps one to feel successful. Wearing Prada shoes and carrying a matching Prada handbag may help one to fill self-assured and prestigious.

Brand managers often differentiate their brands by emphasizing that their brands can satisfy a need better than other brands. The successful brand manager must make sure that the key benefits a target audience wants are satisfied much more with the brand manager's brand than with a competing brand. To achieve this, the brand manager must understand a target audience's needs and the degree to which the brand satisfies those needs compared to competing brands.

5.0 Conclusion

To the casual reader, devoting time to understanding and distinguishing the various brand concepts may not seem to be very important. Practitioners are often most concerned with attaining those desired outcomes we discussed earlier. Learning the meaning of various brand concepts may seem to be an impractical academic exercise. However, failing to adequately understand brand concepts or misuse brand concepts leads to confusion, miscommunication, and lowered effectiveness. If you as a leader cannot explain to those who develop marketing plans and to those who implement marketing plans what you want with precision, you should not be surprised if *your* desired marketing objectives are not attained.

For example, when a manager indicates he or she is concerned about increasing brand loyalty, what does this really mean? Is the manager referring to customer retention, stimulating repeat purchases in the future, or the level of devoted attachment customers feel toward the branded product or the marketing organization? Unless we are precise in our identification of what our desired marketing outcome variables are, the plans that we develop to attain the outcomes will be less valid and less effective.

It would be useful for marketing professionals to define the terms they use. This is especially important when a term has both a proper meaning in our language and a different meaning in industry jargon—like loyalty. For example, when a manager indicates that he or she wants a specified increase in customer loyalty, he or she should explain to what customer loyalty refers. If the manager is using the term loyalty to refer to customer retention or future patronage, it would be better to use those terms instead of loyalty. Likewise, if a manager really wants to increase customer loyalty, then because the term is often misused to refer to other concepts, the manager should define the term. For example, if you want to increase customer loyalty by 10% next year, you might say "We want to increase customer loyalty by 10% by year's end. By loyalty, we are referring to our customers' sense of devoted attachment to our product brand." Hence, other marketing professionals will have greater clarity in understanding the marketing outcomes they are expected to attain. If marketing planners do not have a clear understanding of what variables they are expected to change, they will be less effective.

If you, as a marketing professional, are communicating with a superior or subordinate who is imprecise in using terms, it would be prudent to verify that the two of you share the same understanding of the marketing variables you are discussing.

Key Terms

Brand	Brand, used as a verb, (as in *to brand*) refers to placing an identity on a target object. Brand, used as a noun, refers to a target group or audience's comprehension of the branded object.
Brand identifiers	Brand identifiers refer to brand attributes (e.g., name, logo, symbol, or other distinguishing features) that are used to identify or distinguish a brand object.
Brand attributes	Brand attributes refers to the nature, characteristics, or qualities of the branded object. Brand attributes are components or elements of the brand object.
Brand management	Brand management refers to the development and implementation of plans pertaining to the brand object.
Brand management tactics	Brand management tactics or activities refer to the specific activities that will be implemented throughout the year in order to achieve the goals and objectives.
Brand object	Brand object refers to the entity that is the target of branding (or brand identification).
Brand orientation	A brand orientation refers to a type of marketing orientation that emphasizes the achievement of

organizational goals through managing the organization's brand.

Brand positioning	Brand positioning refers to an aspect of brand management strategy that pertains to decisions about how managers want their brand perceived by a target group.
Brand promotion	Brand promotion refers to managerial activities to communicate to a target group with respect to the brand.
Brand strategy	The brand strategy refers to the general approach used to achieve the brand goals and objectives.
Goal	A goal refers to desired managerial outcomes.
Marketing orientation	Marketing orientation refers to a mindset, way of thinking, or tendency to predominately view organizational issues from a marketing perspective.
Peer brands	Peer brands refer to those other brands audiences consider to be alternatives to a target brand.
Purpose of marketing	The purpose of marketing is to attract support to the organization.
Support	Support refers to the desired response a marketer is seeking from a target audience or group.

3 BRANDING STRATEGIES

After reading this chapter you should:

1. Understand brand, branding, and brand management.

2. Understand brand strength, its dimensions, and how it is measured.

3. Understand how a long-term brand strategy increases the effectiveness of annual marketing and communication activities

4. Understand the relationship between continuous improvement and brand management.

1. Introduction

It is important to keep in mind that marketing and branding are means to an end. This means that the reason organizations use marketing and branding is to achieve desirable outcomes. The purpose of marketing is to attract support to the organization. Branding is one pathway of attracting the desired support to the organization.

Monopoly control over a necessity does not need to use marketing. Examples of monopolies of necessities are utilities (e.g., electricity, water, sewage removal) and life-saving patented prescription drugs. There is a demand for these necessities. There are no or very few accessible alternatives for consumers.

The more alternatives supporter groups (consumers, donors, voters)

43

have, the more marketing and branding are needed to attract support to organizations. When potential supporters (consumers, volunteers, donors, voters, etc.) have multiple alternatives, marketing is used to communicate to potential supporters why they should support an individual organization rather than alternatives.

The central topic of this chapter is branding strategies. What is the general direction that characterizes the emphasis of our branding activities (tactics). The brand strategy is a plan for the entire brand program of activities. With respect to brand strategy, there is one central objective—to increase brand strength. Organizations want their brands to become stronger brands. If an organization is the strongest brand among its peer class, it wants to remain the strongest brand.

Since the purpose of a brand strategy is to strengthen the brand, a good portion of this chapter is devoted to developing a deeper understanding of brand strength and its components. Then, the chapter discusses how to analyze a brand and the strategic implications that result from the analysis.

What does it mean to say that a brand is strong? What is brand strength? How does a manager develop and maintain a strong brand? What are the benefits and outcomes of having a strong brand? There has been substantial prior research on the various parts of the brand nomological network (net). However, the absence of conceptualizing and measuring brand strength remains a substantive gap in the literature. While prior research has discussed strong brands in terms of their likely correlates or outcomes, the field has not conceptualized the nature and characteristics of the brand strength construct.

It appears obvious to marketing professionals that it is desirable to have a strong brand. A strong brand is desirable because of the potential benefits that having a strong brand implies. Because brand strength produces favorable marketing outcomes, it was surprising to discover that the conceptualization and measurement of brand strength has received very little attention in prior marketing research, even in articles in which terms like "brand strength" or "strong brands" are used and the importance of strong brands is mentioned (Henderson et al., 2003; Hoeffler & Keller, 2003; John et al., 2006; Keller, 1993).

Biel (1992) argues that marketing scholars have not articulated the underlying characteristics that make a brand strong. Two decades later, the brand strength construct still has not been adequately conceptualized. Mac-Kenzie (2003) finds that failure to adequately specify the conceptual meaning of a study's focal constructs is a common source of invalid research. One purpose of this chapter is to provide a more complete conceptualization of nonprofit brand strength. It seems erroneous to invest in brand management tactics in order to achieve the benefits of a strong brand without first understanding what a strong brand actually is.

Another purpose of this chapter is to conceptualize the moderating role of nonprofit brand strength. The motivation for investing in brand management activities is to achieve the benefits that are believed to be a consequence of having a strong brand. It is, therefore, apparent that brand strength plays a role in the relationship between brand management activities and their desired marketing outcomes or consequents. This role will be discussed in an effort to improve our theoretical understanding of brand strength and its relationship within its nomological net.

2. Conceptualizing brand strength

A brand represents how the public (or a target group of interest) perceives or comprehends the organization (Simoes and Dibb, 2001). "A brand is a psychological construct held in the minds of all those aware of the branded product, person, organization, or movement" (Kylander & Stone, 2012, p. 37). Nonprofit organizations do not typically brand discrete products or services. Instead their brand is derived by a target audience's perceptions of their organizations (Daw & Cone, 2011). Hence, a brand needs to be construed as a target group's comprehension of the organization (Tapp, 1996). Therefore, we define a brand as a target group's comprehension of the organization based on their experiences with the organization and information they have received about the organization (Brown, 1992; Daw & Cone, 2011).

The brand strength construct has an individual as well as a comparative quality. An organization can be a weak brand if it is relatively unknown or if target audiences perceive it to be mediocre. A brand may also be weak or strong, by a target audience's comparison of the organization with its peers (peer brand set). The strength of a brand is based on the perceptions of a target group or audience of managerial interest. This view is consistent with that of Dacin and Smith (1994), who argue that brand strength should be construed from the perspective of a target audience or group. For a consumer product brand, this might be the target consumer group. For a nonprofit organization, this might be the general population or some population subgroup (Helmig & Thaler, 2010). Based on a review of the branding literature, is it argued that a strong brand, compared to a weak brand, has the following properties:

1. A strong brand is well-known to a target group of interest.
2. A strong brand is favorably perceived by a target group of interest.
3. A strong brand is believed to be exceptional and extraordinary in comparison to peer brands by a target group of interest.

2.1 A strong brand is **well-known.**

An organization would want its brand to be well-known to target groups of managerial importance. The characteristic of being well-known refers to how familiar a target group is with a branded object. Napoli (2006) argues that the more well-known a charity brand is, the stronger it is.

Prior research in consumer products branding has recognized the importance of brand familiarity and its probable antecedent relationship to purchase intention, repeat purchase, brand recall, and other consequent variables (Aaker & Keller, 1990; Campbell & Keller, 2003; Hoyer & Brown, 1990; Kent & Allen, 1994; Laroche & Zhou, 1996). Hoeffler and Keller (2003) argue that consumer familiarity (based on ownership, prior knowledge, or brand exposure) has served, in prior research, as a proxy for strong brands.

There is some similarity between brand familiarity and brand awareness. Brand awareness, however, is a construct with limited applicability and which is subsumed into brand familiarity. One is either aware of the brand object or not. It is not descriptive to assess the degree to which one is aware of a brand. For example, what does it mean to say one is very aware of the brand object or merely somewhat aware of the brand object? However, brand familiarity incorporates brand awareness and adds a magnitude facet. For example, if one is not aware of the brand then one is also not familiar with the brand. If one is aware of the brand, the degree to which one is familiar with the brand will vary along a familiarity continuum.

Brand familiarity is a necessary but insufficient component of brand strength. While a strong brand may be one with which an important group is familiar, a familiar brand may be unpopular or disliked (and therefore, weak). It is possible for a familiar brand to be perceived as mediocre in comparison to a peer brand, suggesting the mediocre brand is comparatively weak. Hence, in addition to being a familiar brand, the brand must also be perceived favorably by the target group of interest. This leads into the second characteristic of a strong brand.

2.2 A strong brand is favorably perceived.

Being perceived positively relates to the attitude concept. Since attitude has a valence and a magnitude, attitude is well-suited as a means of assessing the degree of favorability with which the organization or other branded object is perceived by a target audience. Prior research in commercial branding has recognized the importance of brand attitude and its probable antecedent relationship to outcome variables indicative of a strong brand, such as brand equity (Faircloth, Capella, & Alford, 2001; Kardes & Allen, 1991; Keller, 2001; Lane & Jacobson, 1995; Park & Young, 1986; Simonin & Ruth, 1998). Dacin and Smith (1994) argue that the favorability of consumers' brand predispositions is important in conceptualizing brand strength.

Like familiarity, a favorable attitude is a necessary but insufficient component of a strong brand. For example, most well-known charities are perceived favorably by the public. Many charities do good work and enjoy favorable public attitudes. For a charity to be considered the strongest brand in its class, however, something additional is required. Among charities having similar missions and attracting donations and volunteers from the same population, it is the stand-out, exemplar, and best organization which will attract the most support, thus indicating an additional characteristic is also a component of brand strength.

2.3 A strong brand is exceptional and extraordinary in comparison to peer brands.

This brand strength characteristic pertains to how exceptional a target group perceives a brand in comparison with other brands in its class. Brand strength is an interesting concept in that it has a comparative quality. If a community has three similar nonprofit organizations, the organization with the greatest brand strength would be perceived as exceptional in comparison with the other two organizations. If an organization is viewed as no better than similar organizations, then this perception of being average would imply a brand of average strength. If an organization is perceived as being worse than similar organizations, then one would expect this organization's brand strength to be below average. Prior literature supports the argument that a strong brand needs to be perceived as exceptional and extraordinary (Godin, 2009; Hildreth, 2010; Temple, 2011; Vrontis, 1998). Biel (1992), for example, argues that salience within a product class is a requirement of being a dominant brand. Simoes and Dibb (2001) argue that a dominant brand needs to have some aspect of uniqueness and it needs to be perceived as representing quality. We believe they were referring to the need of a dominant brand (the strongest brand in its class) to be perceived as differentiated and superior in comparison with its peer brands.

Brand remarkability, as a dimension of brand strength, helps to overcome a conceptual error in prior literature that conflated differentiation with superiority. For example, Aaker (1996) argues that differentiation (being different from competing brands) was the essential characteristic of a brand that enabled it to command a price premium. We argue, however, that simply being different is insufficient to make a brand strong. A brand object can be different, but in a negative manner. A brand object can be different, but in a manner that does not make it the preferred brand among potential supporters. Hence, remarkability is assessed from the perspective of the target audience or group and refers to the extent to which the brand object stands out in an exceptional manner from peer brands.

2.4 Construct Definitions.

Based on the preceding discussion and literature review, brand strength is defined as the degree to which a brand is well-known to a target group, is perceived favorably by a target group, and is perceived to be remarkable in comparison to peer brands by a target group. Hence, brand strength is conceived as having three dimensions: brand familiarity, brand attitude, and brand remarkability. Brand familiarity refers to the level of knowledge the target audience has about the brand object. Brand attitude refers to the degree to which a brand object is perceived favorably by a target group. Brand remarkability refers to the degree to which a brand object is perceived by a target group to be extraordinary.

3. Brand strength as a moderator

The purpose of marketing is to attract support to the organization. Hence, marketing tactics, if successful, should increase support for the organization. For a business, support might come in the form of increased sales; for a politician, increased votes. For a membership organization, support might be manifested by increased member retention or recruitment. For a charity, support might be manifested by increased donations.

This cause and effect relationship is perhaps too simple because increased levels of marketing activities do not always result in increased support. Marketing activities have to be appropriately planned and implemented to result in increased support. Therefore, other constructs are present in the marketing activities → marketing outcomes nomological net. In Figure 1, a simple cause and effect (antecedent – consequent) nomological net is presented.

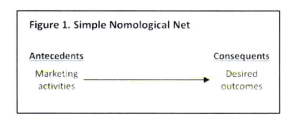

Figure 1. Simple Nomological Net

Referring to Figure 1, marketing activities are seen as a bundle of antecedents which have influence on our target audiences, resulting in some level of the outcomes we hope to achieve from our marketing efforts. In Figure 2, we have a more specific example in which our antecedents are represented in a fundraising campaign and our consequents are represented in the donations (individual contributions) we have attracted from the campaign.

Figure 2. Fundraising Nomological Net

All things being equal, a well-known organization enjoying an excellent reputation (i.e., a strong brand) should receive more donations than an unknown organization or an organization with a poor reputation (i.e., weak brands). Hence, brand strength appears to have a moderating influence on the relationship between the fundraising campaign and the resultant contributions. Brand strength, as a moderator, is depicted in Figure 3.

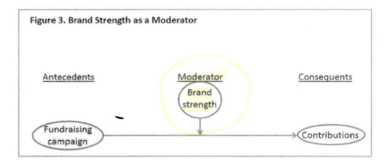

Referring to Figure 3, the moderator, brand strength, influences the strength of the relationship between the antecedent (exogenous) and consequent (endogenous) constructs. Brand strength is measured as a continuous (interval) variable. Brand strength influences the strength of the influence of the antecedent on the consequent. As brand strength increases, the fundraising campaign becomes more effective (has greater influence on contributions).

4. Brand strength's inter-dimensional dynamics

Brand strength is conceptualized as having three dimensions: brand familiarity, brand remarkability, and brand attitude. The three dimensions are distinct, but are obviously inter-related. The conceptual domain of brand strength is depicted in Figure 4 to illustrate the inter-dimensional relationships.

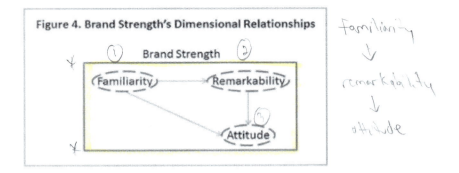

Figure 4. Brand Strength's Dimensional Relationships

In providing an inter-dimensional theory of brand strength, it must be remembered that brand strength is a psychological construct. Brand strength is derived from the perceptions of individuals from groups of managerial importance. With respect to Figure 4, brand familiarity is presented as the prime mover. If an organization is unknown to a target audience (i.e., familiarity = 0), members of the target audience are unable to form perceptions of brand remarkability and brand attitudes. Once a target audience has some level of familiarity with the organization, perceptions of remarkability are formed. Brand attitudes are formed last in our temporal sequence. Attitudes have a valence (polarity) and magnitude (strength). Familiarity is the primary influencer of attitudinal magnitude; remarkability is the primary influencer of attitudinal valence. The inter-dimensional theory of brand strength has managerial implications, which will be discussed next.

5. Brand strength's managerial implications

Understanding the inter-dimensional theory of brand strength informs brand management planning. Managerial emphasis is best placed on increasing familiarity and remarkability. Attitudes are derived from familiarity and remarkability, making the great attention placed on attitudes in prior literature of questionable value.

With the goal of having a strong brand, managerial emphasis should begin with creating an exceptional organization (high remarkability), and then this remarkability can be embedded in communications activities that increase audience familiarity with the organization. If managers have not begun with this brand-orientated emphasis, then they can assess their current brand strength status as a diagnostic tool for informing subsequent brand management strategies. This is illustrated in Figure 5.

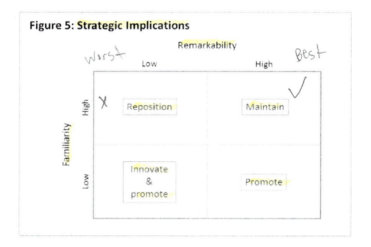

Figure 5: Strategic Implications

In Figure 5, a four-cell grid is presented in which remarkability is placed on the horizontal axis, and familiarity is placed on the vertical axis. Each dimension (i.e., remarkability and familiarity) is partitioned into high and low conditions. Hence, an organization, depending on its brand strength dimension scores in comparison with its peers, can be placed into one of the four cells or quadrants.

The upper right quadrant in which the organization is well-known and remarkable is the most desirable position. This organization is a strong brand. The brand strategy should be to maintain its strong brand position. The organization should practice continuous improvement management, ensuring that stakeholder groups' perceptions are guiding the direction of improvement. The organization should also have a regular program of communication with stakeholder groups and potential supporters.

In the bottom right quadrant, the organization is remarkable (or would be perceived as such if more people were familiar with the organization), but is little known. In this situation, the marketing strategy should place an emphasis on promoting the organization to target audiences so that the level of familiarity with the organization among target audiences increases. Greater familiarity should result in a strong brand (the upper right quadrant), in which case the marketing strategy will shift to a maintenance strategy. The key difference between the maintenance and promotion strategies is that the promotion strategy involves a more intensive communication program.

In the bottom left quadrant, target audiences are unfamiliar with the organization. However, if they were more familiar with organization they would perceive it as relatively unremarkable. The strategy should be to first improve the organization to increase its remarkability (innovation). Once a substantial level of remarkability has been achieved, then an intensive program of communication to target audiences can begin to increase familiarity with the organization (promotion). Obviously the communication messages will describe the organization's remarkability. Once the brand has become strong (moved to the upper right quadrant), a shift to a maintenance strategy is appropriate.

In the upper left quadrant, the organization is well-known (high familiarity), but is regarded to be unremarkable. Although it may appear to be advantageous to have a high level of familiarity, this quadrant is the least desirable with respect to marketing strategies. Because the organization is well-known, target audiences have formed an understanding of the organization that is relatively fixed and enduring. Changing existing audience beliefs from unfavorable to favorable is a challenging task. This marketing strategy is called repositioning. Audiences must be convinced that the organization has undertaken major improvements. Successful repositioning requires major organizational changes (which may involve operational changes and leadership changes). Once the major improvements have resulted in an organization that will be perceived to be remarkable, an intensive communication program featuring the metamorphosis of the organization can be undertaken. A repositioning strategy is sometimes accompanied by an organizational name change to signal to target audiences that the organization is substantially renovated that it can be considered to be a different organization.

5.1 Target audience perceptions

Brand strength is an interesting construct. Brand strength is a psychological construct. It is the collective perceptions of a target audience of importance to the marketing organization. Furthermore, brand strength relates to perceptions of the organization. Since target audiences also have perceptions of other (peer) brands that are similar to the organization, brand strength is comparative. A brand is only as strong as it is perceived in comparison to its peers by target audiences. Figure 5 depicts this situation.

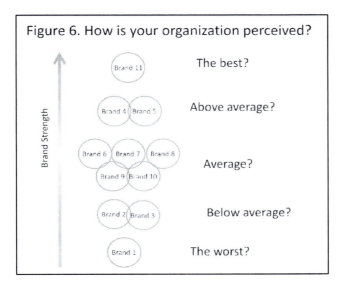

Figure 6. How is your organization perceived?

As Figure 5 illustrates, a brand is comprehended in relation to its peers. Most brands will be perceived to be about average, similar to alternatives. From a marketing perspective being perceived as average means that the brand is perceived to be neither really good nor really bad. Potential supporters from important target audience do not see the organization to be special or exceptional.

For example, let's image that you and a friend visit a fast food restaurant for lunch—Wymer's Hamburger Emporium. This will be your first visit to Wymer's Hamburger Emporium. Many people have eaten meals at fast food chain restaurants and have a good idea of what to expect from the experience. Your experience at Wymer's Hamburger Emporium will be evaluated in relation to your experiences at similar fast food restaurants. All the different attributes of the experience at the Emporium will have some weighting in your evaluation of the experience. Relevant brand attributes for the Emporium (and similar restaurants) might include how modern and well-maintained the facilities appear. They might include the general cleanliness of the restaurant, including the condition of the toilets. The ease of understanding the menu, the pricing, the taste and freshness of the food would likely be other attributes of importance. Other attributes might include the friendliness and apparent skill of the staff, waiting times to place order and receive food. While all these attributes will have some influence in your assessment of Wymer's Hamburger Emporium, (1) some attributes will be more important than others and (2) the degree to which an attribute differs from the average will affect an attributes influence on your overall evaluation of the restaurant.

Continuing with our example, let us imagine that you and your friend found the restaurant acceptable. It was similar in most respects to the major fast food restaurants you have visited in the past. The Emporium may feel good about this evaluation. In fact, the Emporium happily reports that 90 percent of its customers (from customer replies to online surveys) are satisfied. The Emporium may even feature a 90 percent customer approval rating in its advertising messages.

Unfortunately, customer satisfaction is not a very useful measure of customer perceptions. While you and your lunch companion found your experience to be satisfactory, you also did not find anything exceptional or special about your lunch experience at the Emporium. If there is nothing really special about the Emporium, you will probably not be eager for your next meal there. You will probably not recommend Wymer's Hamburger Emporium to your acquaintances. You may not remember the Emporium unless reminded by regular advertising. In the future, when you are choosing a restaurant, the Emporium may not even be considered.

All things being equal, the best brands are remembered, preferred, and supported. The worst brands are remembered, detested, and avoided.

5.2 Managerial perceptions

Most managers do not really understand the perceptions of their target audiences, especially how their brands are comprehended in relation to peer brands. I recall, when I was a doctoral student, a brand manager from a major corporation visited the marketing department. He (they are usually males) wanted some insights from the marketing professors and doctoral students about how to leverage their company's brand equity. In his responses to our questions, he disclosed that he and his colleagues had recently begun to learn more about how consumers were using their home cleaning products by asking managers' wives (did I mention that the executives were males) to use the products at home and let them know how they found the products. This executive had been brand manager of a major corporation for 12 years and had really never thought to understand customers' perceptions! The executive must have limited his information for decision-making to marketing expenses (advertising and promotion expenses) and sales data.

This managerial perception blindness is also prevalent in other types of organizations. For example, I teach a course in nonprofit marketing in which students recruit community nonprofit organizations as clients for a course project. It has been almost always the case that nonprofit managers grossly overestimate how well-known their organizations were in the community.

The reasons for these misperceptions are varied. Corporate managers tend to insulate themselves from customers. There are several layers of organizational management layers which result in executives being far removed from regular interactions with customers. In small businesses, it is often the case that the least rewarded jobs are those in which employees are directly involved with customers. Distance from customers is almost seen to be a benefit for higher status positions.

In community nonprofit organizations, managers often separate them-

selves from important audiences. Managers may find dealing with supporters to be unpleasant and, therefore, to be avoided (tasks for lower level staff
to perform). Managers may find themselves too occupied with meetings,
initiatives, and operations to partition time for regular supporter interaction.

Without regular interaction with members of important target groups,
managers' perceptions are necessarily influenced by other sources. Since
managers spend most of their time with coworkers, family members, and
others in their social networks who know more about the organization than
target audiences, managers tend to overestimate how well-known and how
favorably their organizations are perceived. To correct for this bias, managers must first be aware of the bias, and then to seek out better information
on target audience perceptions. Otherwise, marketing plans will be developed with an incorrect understanding of target audiences.

5.3 Diagnosing poor brand performance

In this book, we provide the reader with a strong theoretical basis for
understanding branding and brand management. When managers have a
strong knowledge base, they have the tools for analysis and the basis from
which to engage in creative innovation. Our approach to brand management is quite practical. For example, if a brand is performing poorly, Figure
7 presents a simple decision framework that can guide brand management
strategy.

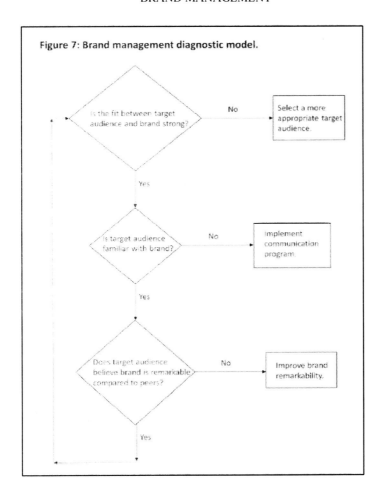

Figure 7: Brand management diagnostic model.

When a brand is performing poorly, the first issue a brand manager should evaluate is the extent to which there is a strong match or fit between the brand benefits and the target audience's needs. Assuming the brand provides a strong mix of benefits, the brand manager should identify a target audience that is a stronger fit for the brand. If the brand manager discovers that the brand cannot outperform peer brands from the perspective of any target audience, then the only recourse is to improve the brand remarkability (the topic of a subsequent chapter of this book).

If the target audience is a good fit for the brand, then the next issue to evaluate is the degree to which the target audience is familiar with the brand. If the target audience is insufficiently familiar with the brand to perceive the fit between the brand's benefits and its needs, then the brand manager should launch a strong communications program to increase brand familiarity (the topic of a subsequent chapter in this book).

If the target audience is quite familiar with the brand, then the remaining issue to be evaluated is the extent to which the brand is perceived to be remarkable. Analyzing brand remarkability and planning corrective actions is the topic of a subsequent chapter in this book. If the brand manager determines at this point (see Figure 7) that remarkability is not deficient, then the brand manager has made a mistake in the analysis and the process depicted in Figure 7 should be repeated.

6. References

Aaker, D. & Keller, K. (1990). Consumer evaluations of brand extensions. *The Journal of Marketing*, 54(1), 27–41.

Aaker, D. (1996). Measuring brand equity across products and markets. *California Management Review, 38*(3), 103-120.

Biel, A. (1992). How brand image drives brand equity. *Journal of Advertising Research*, 32(6), 6–12.

Brown, G. (1992). *People, brands and advertising*. New York, NY: Millward Brown International.

Campbell, M. & Keller, K. (2003). Brand familiarity and advertising repetition effects. *Journal of Consumer Research*, 30(2), 292–304.

Dacin, P. & Smith, D. (1994). The effect of brand portfolio characteristics on consumer evaluations of brand extensions. *Journal of Marketing Research*, 31(2), 229–242.

Daw, J. & Cone, C. (2011). *Breakthrough nonprofit branding: Seven principles to power extraordinary results*. Hoboken, NJ: John Wiley & Sons.

Faircloth, J., Capella, L., & Alford, B. (2001). The effect of brand attitude and brand image on brand equity. *Journal of Marketing Theory and Practice*, 9(3), 61–75.

Godin, S. (2009). *Purple cow: Transform your business by being remarkable*. Miami, Florida: Business Summaries.

Helmig, B. & Thaler, J. (2010). Nonprofit marketing. In Rupert Taylor (Ed.), *Third sector research* (pp. 151-169). New York: Springer.

Henderson, P., Cote, J., Leong, S., & Schmitt, B. (2003). Building strong brands in Asia: Selecting the visual components of image to maximize brand strength. *International Journal of Research in Marketing*, 20(4), 297–313.

Hildreth, J. (2010). Place branding: a view at arm's length. *Place Branding and Public Diplomacy*, 6(1), 27–35.

Hoeffler, S. & Keller, K. (2003). The marketing advantages of strong brands. *Journal of Brand Management*, 10(6), 421–445.

Hoyer, W. & Brown S. (1990). Effects of brand awareness on choice for a common, repeat-purchase product. *Journal of Consumer Research*, 17(2), 141–148.

John, D., Loken, B., Kim, K., & Monga, A. (2006). Brand concept maps: A methodology for identifying brand association networks. *Journal of Marketing Research*, 43(4), 549–563.

Kardes, F. & Allen, C. (1991). Perceived variability and inferences about brand extensions. *Advances in Consumer Research*, 18(1), 392–398.

Keller, K. (1993). Conceptualizing, measuring, and managing customer-based brand equity. *Journal of Marketing*, 57(1), 1–22.

Keller, K. (2001). *Building customer-based brand equity: A blueprint for creating strong brands*, working paper, Marketing Science Institute.

Kent, R. & Allen, C. (1994). Competitive interference effects in consumer memory for advertising: the role of brand familiarity. *Journal of Marketing*, 58(3), 97–105.

Kylander, N. & Stone, C. (2012). The role of brand in the nonprofit sector. *Stanford Social Innovation Review*, 10(2), 35–41.

Lane, V. & Jacobson, R. (1995). Stock market reactions to brand extension announcements: The effects of brand attitude and familiarity. *The Journal of Marketing*, 59(1), 63–77.

Laroche, M., Kim, C., & Zhou, L. (1996). Brand familiarity and confidence as determinants of purchase intention: An empirical test in a multiple brand context. *Journal of Business Research*, 37(2), 115–120.

MacKenzie, S. (2003). The dangers of poor construct conceptualization. *Journal of the Academy of Marketing Science*, 31(3), 323–326.

Napoli, J. (2006). The impact of nonprofit brand orientation on organisational performance. *Journal of Marketing Management*, 22(7–8), 673–694.

Park, C., Young, S. (1986). Consumer response to television commercials: The impact of involvement and background music on brand attitude formation. *Journal of Marketing Research*, 23(1), 11–24.

Simoes, C. & Dibb, S. (2001). Rethinking the brand concept: New brand orientation. *Corporate Communications: An International Journal*, 6(4), 217–224.

Simonin, B. & Ruth, J. (1998). Is a company known by the company it keeps? Assessing the spillover effects of brand alliances on consumer brand attitudes. *Journal of Marketing Research*, 35(1), 30–42.

Tapp, A. (1996). Charity brands: A qualitative study of current practice," *Journal of Nonprofit and Voluntary Sector Marketing*, 1(4), 327–336.

Temple, P. (2011). Learning spaces as social capital. In Anne Boddington and Jos Boys (Eds.), *Re-shaping learning: A critical reader* (pp. 137-146). London: Sense Publishers.

Vrontis, D. (1998). Strategic assessment: The importance of branding in the

European beer market. *British Food Journal,* 100(2), 76–84.

Key Terms

Brand	…refers to a target group's comprehension of the brand object based on their experiences with the brand object and information they have received about the brand object.
Brand attitude	…refers to the degree to which a brand object is perceived favorably by a target group.
Brand familiarity	… refers to the level of knowledge the target audience has about the brand object.
Brand remarkability	… refers to the degree to which a brand object is perceived by a target group to be extraordinary.
Brand strength	…refers to the degree to which a brand is well-known to a target group, is perceived favorably by a target group, and is perceived to be remarkable in comparison to peer brands by a target group.

4 MEASURING BRAND STRENGTH

After studying this chapter you should:

1. Understand the importance of measuring brand strength.
2. Understand brand strength, its dimensions, and how it is measured.
3. Understand the need to measure the change in brand strength over time.
4. Understand the need to measure the brand strength of your closest peer brands.

1.0 Introduction – the case for measuring brand strength

In this chapter I will discuss issues related to measuring brand strength. Unfortunately, many marketing organizations do not measure their brand strength. Prior to my research program that developed a measurement scale for brand strength, there was no direct measure. Some marketing professionals used outcomes of brand strength (like sales, market share, or brand equity) as substitute measures.

Although marketing-oriented organizations want to have strong brands, they often do not measure brand strength. Managers may measure desired marketing outcome variables; like sales, market share, votes, donations, members, or visitors. While measuring brand strength's outcome variables is a good thing to do and provides useful information, these variables do not measure actually brand strength.

One could argue that a specific measure for brand strength is not needed because these other variables can serve as substitutes. Furthermore, since the purpose of marketing is to achieve outcomes, like increased sales, the added expense of measuring brand strength is unneeded. I would argue in favor of also measuring brand strength.

Referring to Figure 1, assume that yours in one of the brands (brands 1-11) depicted. If you only know your own organization's sales level (or other outcome variable), this tells you very little about how strong your brand is. The relative strength of your brand is based on how potential supporters (potential customers or donors, for example) perceive your brand in relation to your peers. When potential supporters think of your brand, they may consider it to be average (most brands are average), better or worse than average, or the best (or worst) brand.

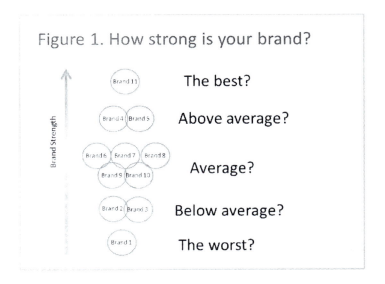

Figure 1. How strong is your brand?

Recalling that the purpose of marketing is to attract support to the organization, assessing marketing outcome variables only, and doing so without considering the context of your peer brands provides managers with limited information for marketing and brand management planning. Assume, for example, that your brand in Figure 1 is brand 1 (the worst). By only examining your own organization's outcome variables, you may not fully appreciate the degree to which your organization's marketing efforts have been ineffective. A manager might reply to this argument that one cannot get outcome measures for the set of peer brands. This may be true. However, you can measure the brand strength of your peer brands. In other words, managers do have the ability to create a comparison chart of their brand and its peer brands.

Managers would naturally want to increase the level of support to their organizations. However, this is a tactical or short-term view. A strategic perspective has an answer for the question: Which position (first, second, third, etc.) do you intend for your brand to achieve at some point in the future (one year, five years)? Thus, taking into account your brand strength, as well as the brand strength of your peers, allows you to have much better information to assess brand management effectiveness and inform brand management planning.

As another example, assume that your outcome measures indicate that your support (sales, donations) increased this year. Can you assume, then, that your brand is getting stronger? The simple answer is no. This is because without knowing the same outcome measures for your peer brands, you really cannot make inferences about your brand strength. If the total support to all organizations in your peer set of organizations increased, then your increase in support may simply be a response to this general increase. If your increase in support is less than the increase experienced by your peer brand set, then your brand may actually be getting weaker. A key point to understand is that the performance of your brand can only be fully understood within the context of your peer brand set.

- The performance of your brand can only be fully understood within the context of your peer brand set.

What if a manager *has* total support information on peer brands. In this case, can outcome measures serve as a substitute or proxy for specifically measuring brand strength? Let us use sales as our outcome measure for this example. If managers know the sales of their organization and the total sales of their peer brand set, then they can determine how their organization is performing against the brand average with respect to sales. If managers know the sales of each of the peer brands, then they can assess how their brand is performing compared with their peer brands (rather than just the peer group average). This can be useful information, of course. However, there are two reasons why this approach is not an adequate substitute for measuring brand strength.

First, while it is true that the strongest brand may have the highest sales levels, there are other qualities to having a strong brand that are not brought to managers' awareness. An increase in sales may be due to an organization's current customers (supporters) buying more. It may be due to the organization's ability to attract new customers from competitors (peer brands). It may be due to price changes. It may be due to reduced competition (fewer peer brands). Effective marketing planning requires sufficient information so that underlying performance patterns of peer brands and the behaviors of supporter groups is detected and understood. While measuring brand strength is not a substitute for outcome measures, brand strength is a manifestation of supporter attitudes and intentions. Brand strength is a leading indicator of outcomes and it should be measured periodically.

- Brand strength is a leading indicator of outcomes and it should be measured periodically.

Brand strength is a leading indicator of supporter behavior because brand strength is determined by supporter groups' perceptions. If your brand strength levels are increasing, this indicates that supporter groups are becoming more familiar with your organization and believe the degree to which your organization is better than your peers is increasing. In this case, supporters will increasingly choose to allocate their support to your organization. Supporter groups' sentiments toward your brand predict their future behavior. Measuring brand strength provides information about future supporter behavior. If brand strength increases, managers can expect support to increase over time. If brand strength remains stable, support should be stable (assuming to total level of support to all peers is stable). If brand strength declines, managers can expect support to decline over time.

Measuring outcome variables assesses supporter behavior that has already occurred. Measuring brand strength assesses supporter sentiments, which influence behavioral intentions, which influence behaviors. Hence, brand strength is a predictor of future behavior.

2.0 Brand strength as a means of assessing marketing performance

Organizations invest resources in marketing tactics and activities to attract support. The way in which marketing tactics influence target audiences to provide support can occur directly or indirectly. Pathways of attracting support, as depicted in Figure 2, may have direct effects, indirect effects, or both. To make these concepts more easily understood, some examples will be helpful.

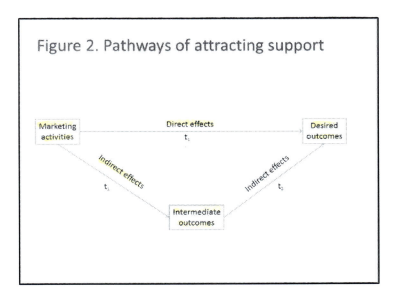

Figure 2. Pathways of attracting support

When marketing activities have direct effects on attracting the desired outcomes, we mean that those activities influenced individuals in the target audience to respond favorably to an appeal for support as a direct consequent of those activities. When individuals viewing a television appeal to send immediate donations to a relief organization (the Red Cross, for example) because of a recent natural disaster, this is an example of the appeal motivating some audience members to donate immediately. Shopping channels on cable television rely on the direct effects of intensive promotion (infomercials) of a specific product in a few minutes. Coupons are a form of advertising that attempts to stimulate a direct effect. That is, individuals receiving a store or restaurant coupon (in a newspaper, online, or in the mail) that use the coupon by its expiration date are providing their support to the store or restaurant as a direct response to receiving the coupon.

One advantage of marketing tactics that have direct effects on attracting support is that it is possible to link the effects of the tactic (cause and effect relationship) on the desired outcomes in a relatively precise manner.

Redeemed coupons can be tracked and linked to sales. A marketing professional implementing a direct-mail fundraising campaign for a charity can calculate expenses and compare those expenses to donations resulting from the fundraising appeal. It is interesting to note that these examples of direct effects may also have delayed indirect effects. By indirect effects, I am referring to delayed effects from marketing tactics seeking to attract support that occur through mediating or intermediating variables (factors). For example, if I notice a coupon for McDonalds in a local newspaper and use it the next day I am being directly influenced by the coupon. However, if I enjoyed my meal (and total experience) at McDonalds, my attitude towards McDonalds and my familiarity with McDonalds will increase. This increase in familiarity and attitude may influence my future restaurant choices, representing an indirect effect. Thus, a tactic having a direct effect in the near term (t_1) may also have an indirect effect in the longer term (t_2).

Remaining with the McDonalds example, it is likely that marketing professionals will record expenses related to the coupon tactic (campaign) and compare those expenses to increases in sales that occurred during the time period beginning when the coupons were presented to audience members until the expiration date printed on the coupons (typically about 30 days). It is unlikely that McDonalds' marketing team will be able to link future sales to indirect effects from the coupon campaign. It is also unlikely that the marketing team will be able fully assess the direct effects of the coupon campaign because some outcomes that are desirable are difficult to measure.

Some key points to emphasize are:

1. Marketing tactics may have a direct effect on attracting support (achieving desired outcomes).
2. There may be some desired outcomes that are not anticipated or measured (unaccounted).

3. Marketing tactics may have direct effects on outcome variables and on mediating variables.

4. Direct effects on mediating variables have a subsequent direct effect on their outcome variables.

5. Indirect effects may be unknown to marketing professionals.

6. Indirect effects are often difficult to measure with precision, making their linkage to marketing tactics more difficult to assess.

7. Only a limited proportion of situations lend themselves to linking specific marketing tactics to specific outcomes.

8. Direct effects combined with indirect effects represent the total effects of a marketing tactic.

With respect to the second point listed above, it is obvious but often forgotten that many positive consequences from marketing tactics are overlooked, unobserved, or difficult to measure. Audience attitudes are an obvious example. The ease at which a brand name comes to mind is another example. Marketing tactics that remind audience members of the brand and its favorable qualities may act like a stone tossed into water, creating ripples extending for some distance. Supporter retention is quite important. Marketing tactics that help keep supporters retained are valuable, although the influences on supporter retention are shared among many sources (different marketing tactics) and occur over extended periods of time.

Hopefully, it is apparent to the reader that the effectiveness of marketing activities is difficult to assess and likely to be under-estimated. This has implications for the funding of marketing activities, which will be discussed in the next chapter.

Brand strength is presented in this chapter as an important intermediary variable. In some ways, brand strength represents a composite of audience reactions to prior marketing activities. As a brand gets stronger over time, it has a leveraging effect. That is, a strong brand is the result of effective prior marketing activities, but brand strength positively influences current marketing activities in the near term. Furthermore, brand strength assesses audience's feelings and perceptions of the brand within the context of the peer brand set. Hence, brand strength is an important variable to measure and track.

3.0 Measuring brand strength

Brand strength is easily measured. In Table 1, nine scale items (statements for inclusion in a survey) for measuring brand strength are presented. In the table, the brand object is WWF. In practice, WWF would be replaced with the relevant brand name. Three scale items are used to measure each of brand strength's three dimensions. Therefore, each brand strength dimension can be measured as well as brand strength, itself.

Table 1.
Scale items for measuring brand strength

Familiarity

1. I am knowledgeable about WWF's activities.
2. I am able to describe WWF to others.
3. I have a good understanding of what WWF has done in the past.

Remarkability

4. No organization is better than WWF at doing what it does.
5. WWF really stands apart as being exceptional.
6. WWF stands out in comparison to others.

Attitude

7. I have positive thoughts when I think of WWF.
8. I like WWF.
9. I have a positive impression about WWF.

For valid brand strength measurement, an appropriate sampling of relevant target audiences is selected for a survey. Assuming a near-random procedure for selecting the sample, a good sample size for generating valid results will range considerably depending on the total size of the target audiences. Interested readers can find more information about sample size determination in most statistics books or online searchers using keywords such as "determining sample size" or similar wording. A reasonable sample size would range from 150 for a small community to 1,500 for a national target audience. If an organization has multiple target audiences, separate samples should be taken from each target audience.

The nine scale items for measuring brand strength can be included in a survey. Most organizations would also include measures for additional variables of interest in a survey. The survey platform for data collection could be an online questionnaire, a telephone survey, or a mail survey. Of the three examples, online questionnaires are generally the least expensive.

The brand strength statements presented in Table 1 are known as Likert scale items. This means that for each statement, respondents (persons from the sample who are completing the survey) are asked to indicate their level of agreement (on a scale of 1 to 7, for example). An example is presented in Figure 3.

Figure 3. Likert scale example

Please indicate your level of agreement with the following statement.

1. No organization is better than WWF at doing what it does.

Strongly disagree	Moderately disagree	Disagree	Neither agree or disagree	Agree	Moderately agree	Strongly agree
1	2	3	4	5	6	7

The individual completing the questionnaire would circle one number for each of the nine brand strength scale items (statements) to indicate their level of agreement with each statement. Each person completing the survey would provide one number (1 to 7) for each of the nine statements. Once the surveys are completed, averages are calculated for each brand strength dimension. The average for brand strength, using all nine statements, is also calculated.

Table 2 provides an example of a data set from a sample of 150 individuals from one of an organization's target audiences.

Table 2. Example data for measuring brand strength								
	Familiarity			Remarkability			Attitude		
Case No.	Item 1	Item 2	Item 3	Item 4	Item 5	Item 6	Item 7	Item 8	Item 9
1	2	4	1	2	4	3	1	3	5
2	6	5	7	5	6	4	7	5	6
3	3	4	2	5	4	6	4	5	3
:	:	:	:	:	:	:	:	:	:
:	:	:	:	:	:	:	:	:	:
150	4	5	5	3	5	4	2	5	4
Item Ave	3.2	2.7	3.6	4.1	3.7	2.8	4.3	5.1	4.1
Dimension Ave	3.3			3.4			4.5		
Brand Strength Ave	3.7								

In the table, case number represents each of the 150 respondents who completed the questionnaire. The remaining column headings represent the nine statements or scale items used to measure brand strength and its three dimensions: brand familiarity, brand remarkability, and brand attitude. Each survey participant's responses to the brand strength statements are presented in the rows adjacent to the participant's respective case number. Averages (means) for each variable (brand strength scale item or statement) are presented as well averages for each brand strength dimension. The last row in the table presents the average of all nine brand strength statements, which is our composite brand strength score. Averages for individuals brand strength statements are not particularly helpful. However, brand strength dimension averages and the composite brand strength score are meaningful for managerial planning.

4.0 Using brand strength measurements for planning

One important question marketing professionals ought to ask is whether or not their organizations are becoming more attractive to potential supporters. The purpose of marketing is to attract support from important audiences. Individuals in these audiences (those groups from whom an organization wants to attract support) have alternatives. Is your organization becoming a more attractive or preferred alternative to potential supporter groups over time? If an organization's marketing tactics are having a positive effect on target audiences, the organization will be perceived to be more attractive and preferred in comparison with alternatives (e.g., competitors). The recommended procedure for making this determination is to measure the organization's (or brand object's) brand strength periodically, perhaps annually.

Figure 4 depicts an example of an organization's brand strength scores, measured annually for a number of years. In this example, brand strength is showing an upward trend. If brand strength is not increasing over time, then there is a problem with the effectiveness of the organization's marketing efforts. One potential source of underperforming marketing tactics might be that the brand is the strongest brand in its peer brand set (the focal brand and its closest peer brands). This, of course, would be the result of an organization's marketing efforts performing so well that future increases in brand strength are very difficult to achieve because the brand strength is already very high. This fortunate circumstance is indicated by very high brand strength scores (e.g., 6 to 7 range), especially when the brand's closest peers' brand strength scores are substantially lower (e.g., below 4). Marketing activities for the dominant brand (strongest brand in its peer brand set) would best understood, then, in terms of maintaining the favorable brand strength position within the context of a competitive peer brand set. The dominant brand situation, however, is likely atypical and not the norm. In the more typical case, additional information can be helpful to managers in understanding influences on the performance of marketing activities.

Figure 4. Tracking brand strength

Examining the trend for brand strength dimension scores can help managers better understand the effects of marketing activities on target audiences. Examining the trends of brand strength scores (and dimension scores) of peer brands can also help managers better understand the effects of their marketing efforts on target audiences in the context of peer brands.

Figure 5 presents an example in which the brand strength scores of a focal brand, Brand A, and its closest peer brands, Brand B and Brand C, have been measured over time. Without the comparative peer brand information, Brand A's manager would see that brand strength for Brand A declined sharply in the second year, but the brand recovered its strength by the fourth year.

From the perspective of Brand A, something happened in the second year that reduced its brand strength. However, fortunately the brand has recovered and has shown strong increases in brand strength. Brand A's manager would probably not perceive a need to change marketing tactics. When brand strength measures for Brand A's closest peers, brands B and C, are included as additional information Brand A's manager has an enriched understanding of how target audiences are responding to the marketing activities of the peer brand set. For example, from the first to the second year, the greatest changes were that Brand A's brand strength declined sharply and Brand B's brand strength increased sharply (while Brand C's brand strength remained stable). Perhaps Brand B intensified its marketing activities and potential supporters perceived Brand B to be more preferable than Brand A for this period of time. It is also worth observing that Brand C's brand strength did not decline in the second year and increased substantially in the third and fourth years. Brand C and been getting stronger in comparison with Brand A and is the strongest brand in the peer brand set in the fourth year.

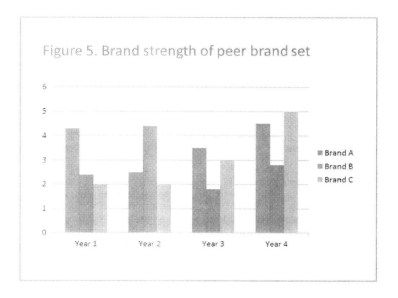

In considering the example presented in Figure 5, we observe that the competitive position of the peer brands is dynamic rather than stable. In other industries, the peer brand set may be quite stable over time. We also observe that interpreting changes in brand strength over time is informed by having information about peer brands. It is also quite helpful to examine brand strength dimension scores for a brand and its closest peers. In the previous chapter, the implications for strategic marketing planning from brand strength dimension scores were discussed. Another example is presented in Figure 6.

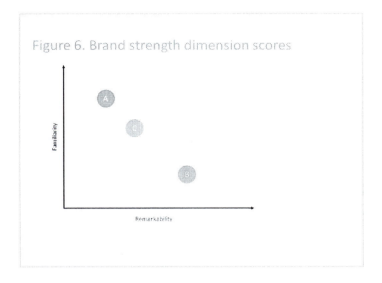

In Figure 6, we show a two-dimensional (familiarity and remarkability) representation of a three-brand peer brand set. A third dimension (attitude) could have been added by varying the size of each brand's circle based on their brand attitude dimension scores. Because brand attitude is strongly influenced by familiarity and remarkability (this issue is discussed in the previous chapter), adding the additional attitude dimension does not add substantial additional information for marketing planning. Referring to Figure 6, we observe that Brand A appears to be very familiar to the target audience, but Brand A is not perceived to be very remarkable. The implication is that Brand A's organization has been implementing marketing activities, evidenced by the high familiarity score. Unfortunately, target audiences perceive Brand A's peers to be superior. The level of brand strength that marketing activities have produced for Brand A have been largely the result of increasing familiarity with the brand object. Target audiences' brand preference for Brand A is restricted by the perceived inferiority (lower remarkability compared to its peers) of Brand A. Does the Brand A manager believe that Brand A is actually inferior to its peers? If so, then the reasonable way to make Brand A stronger is to improve its performance in a way that is meaningful to target audiences (the topic of Chapter 6). If Brand A's manager believes the brand is actually superior to its peers, but that target audiences do not understand this, then the marketing communications directed to Brand A's audiences need to explain why the attributes of Brand A make it superior to its peers. If this strategy proves ineffective, then Brand A's manager's perceptions need to be corrected rather than audience perceptions. If Brand A's manager believes the brand is, in fact, inferior, and then a program of improving the brand object is required.

With respect to the position of Brand B in Figure 6, we see that the target audience perceives it to have low levels of familiarity coupled with relatively high levels of remarkability. The reader may inquire how survey respondents' evaluation of remarkability can be high when they are unfamiliarity with the brand object. This is a valid issue. It would be quite unusual for a brand to have low levels of familiarity and high levels of remarkability because the audience that has little knowledge of a brand (low familiarity) would be expected to find the remarkability of the brand little better than average (how would they know otherwise?). However, it would be valuable for managers to know how remarkable audience members would perceive the brand *if they were more familiar with it*. To get this information from the data, the person analyzing and interpreting the survey data has options. One option is to calculate the average remarkability score for those survey respondents who are familiar with the brand. For example, separate those individuals (cases) who gave responses 5, 6, or 7 (see Figure 3) for each of the three brand familiarity scale items (statements; see Table 2). Then calculate brand remarkability dimension averages for the group of respondents who are familiar with the brand. This remarkability dimension score is the one, then, that can be used in an analysis such as that presented in Figure 6.

(It is a good practice to explain this procedure in any report or presentation of the data analysis.) With such an analysis as this, the reader can interpret the relative extent to which a low remarkability score is influenced by a low familiarity score.

If the reader prefers a more statistical approach to assessing the influence of familiarity on remarkability, a regression analysis may be suitable. A regression analysis uses data from the entire sample, effectively using more information from the data. A relatively simple and robust way to assess remarkability when the familiarity dimension is low is to conduct a regression analysis.

4.1 A regression analysis example

In performing a regression analysis to assess the relationship between familiarity and remarkability, we are finding an answer to the following question: Does remarkability increase if familiarity increases? In the regression, remarkability is our dependent variable and familiarity is our independent variable. The regression analysis tells us two things. First, it lets us know whether or not remarkability increases if familiarity increases. Second, it lets us know the degree to which familiarity influences remarkability.

There are a variety of different software applications which allow a regression analysis of the survey data. Regardless of the application used, typical information reported by the software is presented in Table 2. In the regression analysis familiarity (our independent or predictor variable) is regressed on remarkability (our dependent or criterion variable). In Table 2, the B coefficient (or slope) tells us that remarkability increases 0.75 points (remember we have a seven point scale) for each one point increase in familiarity. SE in Table 2 represents the standard error. (The standard error is the standard deviation of the sampling distribution of a statistic.) Beta is the standardized version of the B coefficient. This means that the B coefficient has been converted to a format that is free of value units and the data has been converted to a standard normal distribution. (If the independent and dependent variables are measured using different scales, it can be quite difficult to interpret the meaning of the B coefficient.) You would interpret Beta thus: a one standard deviation increase in familiarity results in a 0.371 increase in remarkability.

Table 2. Regression analysis results

B	SE	Beta	t value	p value	R^2	Effect size assessment
.750	.109	.371	6.9	.000	0.37	Strong
Notes:	Familiarity = independent (predictor) variable Remarkability = dependent (criterion) variable Effect size criteria ($R^2 > 0.10$, weak; $R^2 > 0.20$, moderate; $R^2 >$ 0.35, strong)					

Next, we examine the t value and p value. They tell us whether or not we can be confident that our results are potentially the result of statistical chance (meaningless). The t value is a statistic produced by dividing the B coefficient by SE. The p value indicates the probability that the t value is less than an acceptable level that our results are not the result of statistical chance (not likely to be a true finding). Typically, if the p value is less than 0.05, we can have confidence that the relationship between familiarity and remarkability is, in fact, genuine, and not a statistical anomaly.

A p value that is less than 0.05 lets us know that a relationship between familiarity and remarkability exists. However, it tells us little about the strength of that relationship. To better understand the degree to which familiarity influences remarkability, we need to assess the effect size of familiarity on remarkability. R^2 (R square) is our effect size measure. It tells us the extent to which respondents answers to the remarkability scale items is influenced by their answers to the familiarity scale items. The R^2 value of 0.37 indicates that 37 percent of the variation of data for remarkability is accounted for by familiarity. Interpreting the strength of this relationship is a somewhat controversial topic in the academic community. For our purposes, an R^2 that is between 0.10 and .020 represents a weak relationship. An R^2 that is between 0.20 and 0.35 represents a moderate relationship. An R^2 that is greater than 0.35 represents a strong relationship. From a practical perspective, what this means is that the greater that R^2 is, the more confidence the reader can conclude that if brand familiarity was high, brand remarkability would also be high.

5 FUNDING MARKETING

After studying this chapter you should:

1. Understand the significance of marketing as a means achieving desired marketing outcomes.

2. Understand the need to hold marketing accountable.

3. Understand the importance of providing sufficient funding for an organization's marketing activities.

4. Understand the source of bias that leads to under-funding marketing.

5. Understand how to correct for the under-funding bias.

6. Understand basic principles for establishing a marketing budget.

1.0 Marketing is a means to an end

The purpose of marketing is to attract and retain support. In the first chapter, I discussed this concept in detail. To a business support means customer patronage. To a city government, this might mean tourism. To a charity, support might refer to contributions from donors. To a politician in an election campaign, support might refer to votes, donations, and volunteering.

An organization that does not need to attract support (perhaps because the organization is a monopoly) does not need to invest in marketing. Such an organization might be the sole provider of a needed product or service. For those organizations that *do* need to attract support, marketing activities are implemented for the purpose of attracting and retaining the needed support.

The reason I make this point is because some organizational decision makers do not understand the purpose of marketing. This misperception influences the role of marketing in the organization. Instead of understanding the important link between marketing and attracting support to the organization, some organizations view marketing as a supportive ancillary function that is subordinated to organizational productive operations. In these organizations, marketing (the managerial function in existence to attract and retain support) is given a low priority—and funded accordingly.

2.0 Hold marketing accountable

Marketing can easily be held accountable because it exists to attract and retain support. If the marketing activities are not achieving the objectives for which they are designed to achieve, then managers can look for the causes of this ineffectiveness. Often the causes are complex. Objectives can be unrealistic. The marketing strategy or tactics can be incorrect for the desired objectives. The marketing tactics can be poorly implemented.

Poor marketing performance may be caused by events external to the organization. For example, a competing organization may implement changes or intensify marketing efforts to which supporters respond favorably. Economic circumstances may vary, affecting target audiences' motivation or ability to support the organization.

In some cases, however, organizations experience poor performing marketing management because of a lack of sufficient funding required to achieve marketing objectives. The purpose of this chapter is to discuss funding marketing activities in an organization. Brand management and branding activities are a part of marketing and are, therefore, affected by organizational funding.

3.0 Consequences of incorrect funding levels

In theory, there is an optimal amount of funding an organization can invest in marketing. For an organization, there is a level of marketing funding that produces the maximum benefits for the funding level provided. Providing more funding than this theoretical optimum amount results in marketing that underperforms for the funding provided. Money is wasted. Providing less funding than this theoretical optimum amount results in marketing that underperforms because of insufficient resources. Support that could have been attracted or retained is lost. Hence, over-funding or under-funding marketing results in underperformance that reduces organizational success.

- Over-funding or under-funding marketing results in underperformance that reduces organizational success.

Most organizations fail to appropriately fund (under-fund) marketing. This cause of organization under-performance has several causes. Managers that do not have a marketing oriented perspective usually fail to understand the indirect and long-term benefits that result from sustained marketing. Managers often rely too heavily on accounting reports to influence their decisions. Accounting reports track money flows coming into and going out of the organization. Therefore, managers are quite sensitive to the costs of funding marketing activities. Accounting reports, however, do not show the money that could have come to the organization but did not. When supporters are not attracted or retained because of a lack of marketing investment, the support that could have been provided to the organization is not estimated or taken into account.

- When supporters are not attracted or retained because of a lack of marketing investment, the support that could have been provided to the organization is not estimated or taken into account by most organizations' accounting systems.

I will discuss more on this issue in a following section. A main point to understand is that most organizations fail to appropriately fund their marketing activities. Ironically, while many organizations are hesitant to fund marketing because they perceive marketing to be a nonessential expense, the underfunding of marketing leads to an organization that underperforms. Because marketing is a means to an end (its purpose is to attract and retain support), funding money represent a net gain to the organization until the optimal funding threshold is reached. That is, each unit of money (dollar, euro, pound, etc.) spent on marketing results in a greater level of money (or value of resources if nonmonetary) returned to the organization up to the theoretical optimal funding level.

- Most organizations fail to appropriately fund their marketing activities.

4.0 The optimal funding level

I acknowledge that the optimal funding level is theoretical. The optimal funding level exists, but it is virtually impossible to calculate. There are too many variables that interact within a dynamic environment. We cannot predict precisely how potential supporters will respond to our marketing activities. There are many variables outside of a manager's control (for example, marketing activities of competitors). Hence, managers want to fund marketing at a level that is near the optimum level, even if they cannot know the exact optimum funding amount.

- **Managers should fund marketing at a level that is *near* the optimum level,** even if they cannot calculate the exact optimum funding amount.

I acknowledge that funding is not the only determinant of marketing performance. A marketing manager can ineffectively plan or implement marketing activities. The effectiveness of competing organizations marketing their peer brands can influence the marketing performance of our organization. The skill of an organization's management team influences the effectiveness of that organization's marketing performance. However, the concepts discussed about funding remain valid. All things being equal, under-funding or over-funding marketing decreases organizational performance.

Back to the main topic of this section, the theoretical optimal funding for marketing is found when marginal marketing funding is equal to marginal marketing returns. When adding one more dollar (one more monetary unit) results in only one additional dollar of support, the optimal funding level has been reached.

- **The theoretical optimal funding for marketing is found when marginal marketing funding is equal to marginal marketing returns.**

As a starting point in explaining these concepts, refer to Figure 5.1. Marketing costs (the funding level for marketing) is presented on the horizontal axis. Marketing returns (the support generated from the funded marketing activities) is presented on the vertical axis. A line representing a relationship in which the amount of marketing funding results in an equal amount of support (marketing returns) is presented. For example, $100 spent on marketing would produce $100 in support or returns. The slope of this line is equal to one. That is, a one dollar change in funding produces a one dollar change in support. We will refer to this line, having a slope equal to one, as our threshold line. Notice also that the angle between the threshold line and the horizontal line is 45 degrees.

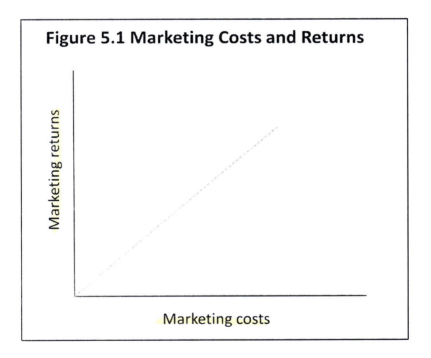

As a practical matter, if an organization's marketing funding and resultant support were equal to the threshold line (slope = 1; 45 degree angle), funding marketing would be irrelevant. If the support generated from marketing were equal to its funding, marketing is not serving a useful purpose for the organization.

Figure 5.2 represents a more typical relationship between marketing costs (funding) and marketing returns (support). Early investments in marketing tend to generate returns far exceeding their costs. Then, as marketing funding continues to increase, the responding increase in support becomes less positive until eventually additional funding results in additional support that is less than the cost incurred in attracting the additional support.

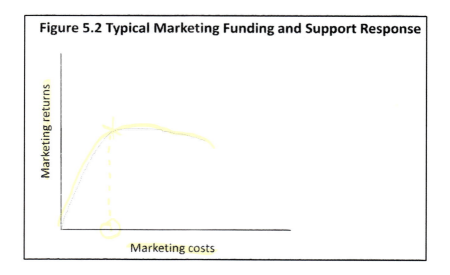

Figure 5.2 Typical Marketing Funding and Support Response

Figure 5.3 presents the optimum marketing funding level. By moving the threshold line upward, while maintaining its slope angle, a point on the typical marketing level and marketing return response curve that has a slope equal to the threshold line can be identified. A vertical dashed line is connects the point on the marketing return versus cost line to marketing costs axis. Point X on the marketing costs axis represents the total marketing funding associated with the point on the typical response curve that has a slope equal to one. The slope of the typical response curve prior to the dashed line is greater than one. The slope of the typical response curve following the dashed line is less than one.

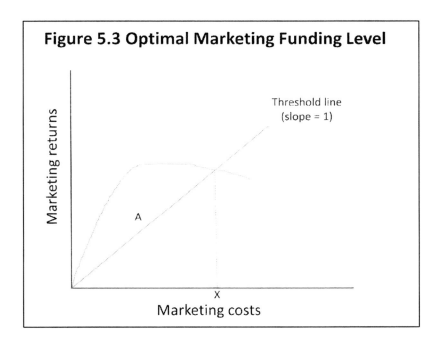

Marketing funding prior to the intersection with the dashed line results in returns greater than their associated marketing costs (slope > 1). The optimal funding level is represented by point X on the marketing costs line. The total returns (support) generated by the optimal funding level is represented by the area under the response curve that is bounded by the dashed line (represented as A under the curve).

Another way to think about the optimal funding level of marketing is that it is productive to fund marketing to the point that additional funding fails to generate benefits (returns, support) that are equal to that additional funding. As long as the funding for marketing produces support that is greater in value to the funding required to generate that support, it is wise to increase marketing funding.

As I discussed previously, it is nearly impossible to accurately forecast the optimum funding level. Even so, it is valuable to understand that there *is* an optimum level. Under-funding or over-funding marketing reduces the effectiveness of the organization. There is, however, a strong bias towards under-funding marketing.

- Under-funding or over-funding marketing reduces the performance of the organization.
- There is a strong bias towards under-funding marketing.

5.0 Measuring costs and benefits (returns)

The primary reason that marketing is typically under-funded in organizations is that managers over-rely on accounting reports to inform their decisions. Accounting reports keep track of the money the organization receives and the money the organization disperses (paying bills, for example). The tracking and reporting of revenues and expenses is conducted in a relatively confined time periods. Usually, revenues and expenses that form the basis of accounting reports are counted monthly and developed into quarterly and annual summary reports.

Accounting reports serve a valuable purpose for managers, enabling them to anticipate the occurrences of cash shortages and providing them with a short-term profit (surplus) estimate. The problem occurs when managers attempt to use accounting reports to inform decisions in areas that are not appropriately measured by accounting reports. This is especially true in the area of marketing management.

5.1 Costs

One reason that organizations under-fund marketing is that the returns generated from marketing costs are under-estimated or not fully measured. Accounting systems place a strong emphasis on measuring expenses. Marketing costs are easily measured. All cash leaving an organization's bank account is carefully tracked by the accounting system. Furthermore, expenses generated for marketing funding are generally experienced in the short-term.

5.2 Returns

Marketing returns (support) are much more difficult to measure than marketing costs. One reason for this difficulty is that returns lag the costs that funded the marketing tactics (that generated the returns). For example, any returns generated from money spent on advertising this month will be realized by the organization only after the advertising has been presented to its audiences. Not only will the returns from advertising occur in the future, they will also be dispersed over time. While managers may believe that above-average revenues occurring in a short period following the advertising represent the returns generated from advertising, advertising effects that generate future returns (delayed effects) will not be linked to the advertising. With respect to delayed effects of marketing activities, the following points are important to remember.

- Returns lag costs
- Returns occur in the short-term and in the long-term
- Returns are generally under-estimated because it is difficult to connect future returns to short-term marketing expenses.

Another reason that it is difficult to measure the returns generated from a specific marketing activity is that there are both direct and indirect effects. Indirect effects are difficult to measure. I will use a restaurant supply company to provide an example. Say, for example, that the restaurant supply company spends $1,000 to advertise in a trade publication read by members of the restaurant industry. Imagine that within 30 days after the advertisement is published a number of product inquiries are made and approximately $1,200 in new orders is generated. Perhaps a discount code number is presented in the advertisement which allows customers to get a 10 percent discount on their orders so that the $1,200 in new orders can be directly linked to the trade journal advertisement.

The $1,200 worth of orders generated by the advertisement represents the direct effects of the advertisement (our marketing tactic or activity). However, there may be indirect effects that are not linked to the advertisement, causing the returns generated from the advertisement to be under-estimated. For example, it is possible that the advertisement increased brand familiarity among a portion of the magazine's readership. Because these customers are more familiar with the supplier, they may be more willing to accept future appointment requests from the supplier's sales representatives. Potential customers may also be more receptive to the supplier's sales representatives because they are more familiar with the supplier because of the advertisement. The increased performance of the sales representatives that is caused by the advertisement is an indirect effect of the advertisement. Hence, the returns generated by the advertisement funding are equal to the direct effects ($1,200) plus the indirect effects (the additional orders through the sales force).

With respect to indirect effects, the follow points are important to remember.

- Indirect effects are those effects of marketing activities that generate additional support (returns) by increasing the effectiveness of another marketing tactic.
- Indirect effects are difficult to measure.

- If indirect effects are not measured or estimated accurately, then the marketing returns generated from a marketing activity are under-estimated.

5.3 Opportunity costs (missed support)

Opportunity cost is an economic term, unfortunately named, that refers to additional revenues (returns, benefits) that an organization would have attracted if it had done something that it did not do (the lost opportunity). Opportunity cost is really referring to lost returns. These lost returns are caused by ineffective management decision-making and are generally not measured in organization accounting systems.

Opportunity costs are losses experienced by the organization because it failed to take advantage of an opportunity. For example, if a hypothetical charity were to hire a professional fundraiser at $80,000/year who could increase donations to the charity by $180,000, the charity experienced an opportunity cost of $100,000 when it decided not to hire the fundraiser. (This is another example of how under-funding marketing causes under-performance.) The accounting system will not identify the opportunity cost (support the organization failed to acquire because it failed to do something.)

5.4 Non-monetary benefits

Marketing goals and objectives do not *always*, nor should they, intend to attract monetary support in the short-term. Non-monetary support is generally not measured by the typical accounting system. Acquiring a new supporter is an example. Marketing activities needed to attract a new supporter often exceed any short-term monetary support provided by the new supporter. An accounting system will track any financial support provided by the newly acquired supporter. However, the value of the new supporter to the organization is ignored.

A charity's fundraising campaign may target individuals who have not previously donated to the charity. If the charity spends $1,000 on a fundraising campaign and generates $900 from the campaign it may conclude that funding and implementing the campaign was a poor decision. However, if the future donations of the newly acquired donors were accurately estimated and included in the analysis, funding the campaign might be perceived as a very wise decision. Further benefits may accrue from the newly acquired donors. For example, the new donors may tell others about the charity (positive word-of-mouth comments and referrals) and they may volunteer for the charity as well.

Supporter (customer, member, donor, or voter) retention is another area in which managers typically grossly under-value marketing returns. Supporters discontinue supporting an organization for a variety of reasons. In many cases, supporters find their experience with an organization to be disappointing or they find their experience with a competing organization (peer brand) to be more rewarding. Spending money that improves supporter experiences and helps to retain supporters is an area of great importance that is often overlooked by managers.

It is generally much more expensive to acquire a new supporter than it is to retain a current supporter. Many organizations, however, are more interested in attracting new supporters than retaining existing supporters. There are several reasons for this problem:

1. Organizations usually do not measure supporter retention.
2. The benefits of retaining supporters are usually not estimated, creating an under-valuation of supporters.

3. Managers often fail to understand reasons supporters discontinue their support.

4. Managers often fail to continuously improve supporter experiences.

Public, media, and government relations are other areas in which the marketing returns are important but nonmonetary. The expenses in funding of these areas of marketing are tracked in an organization's accounting reports. However, improving public attitudes, media attention, and influencing policy makers are nonmonetary outcomes. Increasing public familiarity, improving media coverage, and increasing the attitudes of public officials toward the organization may produce future, indirect monetary and nonmonetary effects. However, the undervaluing of the nonmonetary returns from these marketing activities often results in under-funding of these marketing activities that reduce organizational success.

5.5 Correcting the under-funding bias

Many managers lead under-performing organizations because they fail to adequately fund effective marketing programs. Under-funding marketing retards organizational success. Support that could have been provided to the organization is lost.

The primary cause of the bias towards under-funding marketing is that the benefits and returns from marketing are not measured or not understood. Missed opportunities are often not detected. The importance of retaining supporters is often not considered by managers.

To improve managerial effectiveness and organizational success, managers need to be aware of the under-funding bias and take steps to reduce its effects on their decisions. Better measures need to be provided to more fully account for delayed, indirect, and nonmonetary returns. The information gathering, planning, and decision-making systems need to be improved to reduce the number and importance of lost opportunities that would otherwise go undetected or under-valued.

To compensate for the under-funding bias, managers need to factor into the return estimates a weighted adjustment to counter-balance the downward biasing on marketing returns. The degree to which managers believe a marketing activity will generate delayed or indirect effects should influence the degree to which they upwardly correct the marketing activity's returns. For example, a charity that spends $1,000 on a fund-raising campaign that raises $900 may estimate delayed and indirect effects of the campaign and decide to add a 30 percent weighted adjustment to the short-term direct effect of $900. The corrected campaign return estimate then becomes $1,170. Managers using the uncorrected marketing return estimate in their assessment may conclude that the campaign was a poor decision and that a future fundraising campaign should not be funded. Managers using the corrected marketing return would likely arrive at another conclusion.

- Managers that rely on marketing return estimates that do not correct for the under-funding bias will be less effective than if they rely on corrected marketing return estimates.

Managers that begin to correct for the biases discussed previously begin to learn, over time, how to develop more accurate estimates. They learn how to make better marketing decisions. They become more effective managers. The foundation of this learning process is an effective marketing planning and budgeting process that is refined over time.

5.6 Planning and budgeting for marketing

The general process cycle includes the following:

1. Develop organizational objectives for the year.
2. Determine the role of marketing in helping the organization to achieve its objectives.
3. Develop set of marketing objectives to guide marketing program.
4. Develop marketing and communication plans.
5. Measure costs and returns (including a correction for the under-funding bias).
6. Evaluation of required funding.
7. Refine plans and measures each year (establish a virtuous cycle).

5.6.1 Develop organizational objectives for the year

A central concept in this book is that the purpose of marketing is to attract support to the organization (or other branded object). The attracted support enables the organization to further its mission. This is why organizational objectives are often considered to be strategic and marketing objectives are often considered to be tactical. Organizational objectives navigate the focal interest of the entire organization—toward furthering its mission. Marketing objectives involve developing and implementing activities to attract support.

A business organization's mission (the reason the business exists) is to increase the wealth of its owners. A business's objectives specify desired changes that improve the business's ability to increase or maintain its profits.

A nonprofit organization's mission is to provide a benefit to society. There are some nonprofit organizations whose purported benefit to society is disputed. Nevertheless, the government generally does not prevent the chartering of nonprofit organizations whose benefit to society is controversial. A nonprofit organization's objectives specify desired changes intended to help it advance its purpose.

A government organization's mission is to maintain or improve the general welfare of citizens. This is very broad, of course. When government functions are delegated to government branches or agencies with more narrowly-defined missions, they operate to some extent like nonprofit organizations.

Organizational objectives refer to targets the organization intends its actions to attain. There is a time frame associated with the objectives. With respect to annual planning, the objectives are desired to be attained within the annual planning period. The objectives should be numerical; that is, they should be able to be measured. Otherwise, the organization cannot be sure the degree to which the objectives have been attained. Examples of such objectives are presented in the following table.

Table 5.1 Examples of Organizational Objectives

Stated in absolute terms	Stated in proportional terms
Increase sales next year to $1 million.	Increase sales next year by 20%.
Increase total members to 5,000.	Increase total members by 10%.
Increase market share to 67% of total.	Increase market share by 5%.
Open new store in target location.*	Increase annual new store expansion rate by 1%.
Acquire 100 new customers.	Increase the customer acquisition rate by 4%.
Win an election.	
Get a law changed.	
Increase the capacity of food-insecure persons served by the food bank to 1,000/month.	Increase output capacity of food bank by 5%.
Attract 12,000 applicants for university admission.	Increase applications for admission by 6%.

* This objective can be measured because we can determine easily whether or not a new store has actually been opened. (opened = 1; not opened = 0).

Referring to Table 5.1, it is useful to note that objectives can often be stated in either absolute or proportional terms. Objectives that are stated in absolute or proportion terms can be measured. Not all objectives can be stated in proportional terms. In the table, winning an election (an objective of a political organization) and changing a law (an objective of a lobby or activist organization) are not stated in proportional terms because these objectives are not seen as incremental changes from a prior time period. Not winning the election and not influencing a law change are viewed as failures.

Not only does numerical objective setting enable decision-makers to determine the degree to which they have been successful, it helps managers to learn. Successive cycles of planning, implementation, measurement, and analysis enable managers to better understand the capabilities of their organizations and supporter responses to organizational actions. Learning enables managers to become more accurate in setting objectives, developing plans, implementing plans, and improving organizational performance.

5.6.2 Determine the role of marketing in meeting organizational objectives

After the organizational objectives have been determined, those in the organization responsible for marketing have to determine the degree to which attracting and retaining support influence the attainment of the various organizational objectives. Hopefully, marketing professionals have been involved in organizational strategic planning, and, therefore, understand the extent to which attaining the various organizational objectives are dependent upon successful marketing activities. The responsibility of marketing (what is expected of marketing) for attainment of organizational objectives needs to be clearly understood by members of the organization.

5.6.3 Develop set of marketing objectives to guide marketing program

Marketing planners need to arrive at a consensus with other members of the organization about marketing's role in helping the organization to achieve its organizational objectives. Once marketing planners have clarity with respect to organizational performance expectations they have to develop marketing objectives that, when attained, fulfill marketing's responsibilities for achieving organizational objectives.

To make these ideas less abstract, I will use an example of a hospital that wants to create a new diagnostic medicine department to which physicians could refer patients with an unusual set of symptoms, whose diagnosis is beyond the regular experience of a typical physician. One component of creating the new department is a need to acquire a new diagnostic machine that will perform magnetic resonance imaging (MRI). The cost of the MRI machine will be approximately $1.5 million. The marketing professionals at the hospital are expected to raise the funds (support) to purchase the MRI machine. Hence, the marketing group will have to develop a marketing plan for raising $1.5 million in funding.

An important point to make is the following:

- Not all the marketing objectives will be linked directly to organizational objectives.

Generally, the organizational objectives are short-term (annual) objectives. Marketing objectives developed to attract support for meeting short-term organizational objectives are obviously also short-term. A major concept presented in this book is that effective marketing and brand management requires an effective long-term strategy. That is, to attain the long-term objective of becoming the strongest brand in its class (the brand with the greatest brand strength compared to its peer brands) an organization has to incrementally increase its brand strength each year.

As discussed previously in this book, as brand strength increases, the effectiveness of short-term tactical marketing activities also increases. Building brand strength results in delayed and indirect returns, explaining why managers who do not really understand marketing's benefits and marketing metrics and, therefore, make poor marketing decisions that lead to under-performance. Hence, an organization's marketing team should develop two sets of objectives. One set of marketing objectives are linked to helping the organization to meet the objectives in its annual planning scheme. Another set of marketing objectives are linked to building brand strength over the long-term. Example marketing objectives are presented in the following table.

Table 5.2 Examples of Marketing Objectives

Linked to organizational objectives	*Linked to building brand strength*
Increase sales next year to $1 million.	Increase brand strength by 5%.
Increase total members to 5,000.	Increasing brand strength ranking from 3rd position to 2nd position (among 5 member peer brand set).
Increase market share to 67%.	Increase brand strength from 4.1 to 4.5 (on 7 point scale).
Raise $1.5 million for MRI machine.	Become more remarkable than peer brand A across all audience groups.
Acquire 100 new customers.	Increase brand familiarity across audience groups by 10%.
Win an election.	Increase brand remarkability by 8% across audience groups.
Get a law changed.	Increase brand attitude by 5% for audience group C.
Increase the capacity of food-insecure persons served by the food bank to 1,000/month.	Increase brand familiarity for audience B from 3.2 to 5.0 (on 7 point scale).
Attract 12,000 applicants for university admission.	Increase brand remarkability for audience A by 15%.

Note that all objectives in Table 5.2 can be measured. Therefore, the degree to which an objective is attained can be determined. Once the marketing objectives have been determined, the next step is to develop a plan of marketing actions that will be implemented to attain each objective.

5.6.4 Develop marketing and communication plans

A plan needs to be developed to guide the attainment of each marketing objective. Each marketing plan will present a set of marketing actions needed to attain each objective. Each plan will be sufficiently detailed so that the set of marketing actions are clearly understood by the marketing team and can be implemented without a substantial amount of additional work.

General marketing plan templates available online or in most marketing books are not very helpful and really do not apply for many different types of organizations. It is best for marketing professionals to treat each marketing plan as a plan-of-action for attaining each marketing objective. Precisely what will have to be done, when, and by whom? Over time; through learning that occurs from recurring cycles of planning, implementation, and evaluation; marketing professionals can become quite good at developing useful plans that guide effective implementation of marketing activities.

There is usually an individual marketing plan for each marketing objective. When the same set of marketing activities attain more than one marketing objective, it is efficient to have a one marketing plan for the linked objectives (achieving one objective also achieves another objective). After the marketing plans are developed, they are combined into a general marketing program. The marketing program represents all the marketing plans; that is, all the marketing activities an organization will implement to attain its marketing objectives during the year.

5.6.5 Develop budget

Each marketing plan should have its own budget. When planners develop a set of activities to attain a desired outcome, they should also acquire cost estimates of implementing those activities. The budgets for each plan should be combined into a total budget for the organization's marketing program.

As an illustrative example, I will continue to use the hospital example discussed previously. The objective, I will call it Objective A, is to raise $1.5 million to purchase a new MRI machine. The budget for Marketing Plan A (the plan for attaining Objective A) is presented in Table 5.3.

Marketing Plan A would contain all the specific details about each activity. The amount of support each activity is expected to attract will be specified. Specific details about each activity are reported. Each activity would have a detailed estimated cost report that would show the estimated cost of implementing each component of each activity. Table 5.3 represents a simple summary of cost estimates for the activities in Marketing Plan A.

Table 5.3 Marketing Plan A Budget

Activity	Description	Cost ($)
A1	Kick-off event for potential large donors	3,500
A2	Silent auction	1,500
A3	Walk-A-Thon event	1,000
A4	Direct mail campaign	3,000
A5	5k fun run & walk event	1,000
	Total Cost	**10,000**

When the budget is being reviewed, a manager who might question why the direct mail campaign (Activity A4) will cost $3,000 should be able to refer to the section of the marketing plan that presents this activity. Each component of the direct mail campaign should be explained and cost estimates provided. How cost estimates were calculated and any information sources informing cost estimates should be identified.

In funding the marketing plan, the organization not only needs to know the total amount needed to attain Objective A (the budget for Marketing Plan A), but the organization will also need to know *when* the funds will be needed. The financial manager in the organization will need to know when funds are needed in order to make the necessary plans to have the funds available. Since the different components of a marketing plan are implemented at various times (indicated in the marketing plan), the budget section of the marketing plan should include a budget timeline. The budget timeline refers to when the organization will incur the expense of implementing a component of the marketing plan. The budget timeline for Marketing Plan A is presented in Table 5.4

Table 5.4 Budget Timeline for Marketing Plan A

Tasks	Jan	Feb	Mar	Apr	May	
A1		3,500				
A2			1,500			
A3				1,000		
A4				1,500	1,500	
A5					1,000	
Total		3,500	1,500	2,500	2,500	**10,000**

The organization's marketing program is a combination of all it marketing plans. The marketing program budget is a summary of the marketing plan budgets. Table 5.5 presents an example of a simple marketing program budget. In Table 5.5, the total required funding to attain each marketing objective is presented in the rows. The total budget of $10,000 for Marketing Plan A from Table 5.3 is reported in Table 5.5.

Table 5.5 Marketing Program Budget

Objective (Marketing Plan)	Budget ($)
A	10,000
B	8,500
C	12,250
D	925
Total	**31,675**

A budget timeline for the marketing program is a summary of the budget timelines for the organization's marketing plans. Table 5.6 presents a budget timeline for a marketing program. This timeline shows how much funding is needed on a month-to-month basis, across the year, to attain the marketing objectives reported in the various marketing plans. The organization's financial manager will use this information to make sure the organization has sufficient funds to pay its expenses.

Table 5.6 Marketing Program Budget Timeline

Month	Cost	Month	Cost
Jan	6,000	Jul	2,000
Feb	3,750	Aug	2,000
Mar	1,500	Sep	1,500
Apr	5,500	Oct	1,000
May	3,425	Nov	3,000
Jun	2,000	Dec	0

The financial manager should realize that budget proposals are cost estimates. It is reasonable for the financial manager to expect marketing professionals to develop fairly accurate cost estimates. It is not reasonable to expect the cost estimates to be exact. Actual costs may be a little more or a little less than the estimated costs. Financial managers that refuse to allow specific marketing expenses to exceed forecasted expenses by reasonable (minor) amounts create an incentive for the marketing team to inflate their cost estimates in order to be sure the actual expenses will not exceed the forecasted expenses.

5.6.6 Evaluation of required funding

The marketing professionals in an organization will review the marketing plans and revise them in order to make sure that each plan clearly reports a complete, effective, and efficient plan for attaining their objectives. The organization's top manager reviews the marketing program report.

The marketing professionals in the organization will present their report to the organization's top manager and possibly a management team from different functional areas of the organization. The marketing team should be able to clearly and logically present its marketing program proposal.

If top managers in the organization do not believe the organization can fund the entire marketing program, the marketing team should be prepared to revise the marketing program. It is important to realize that other managers in the organization may not have a thorough understanding of marketing. The top manager or the top management team may propose changes that are counterproductive. Marketing professionals should be prepared if they are placed in a situation that leads to poor marketing performance. Organizational culture and executive personalities will vary considerably, making it difficult for me to provide the reader with a precise set of recommendations. However, I want to help the reader avoid being positioned for underperformance.

For example, in the marketing program budget presented in Table 5.5, the marketing program is expected to cost approximately \$31,675. What if the organization's top manager says \$31,675 is too much and that the marketing team can have \$25,000 to implement its marketing program? The marketing team should reply to this situation by asking the top management team which objectives are least important so that the marketing plan(s) for attaining the least important objective(s) can be postponed until a future date when funding is available to achieve those objectives. If top management refuses this suggestion but insists on underfunding the marketing program, the marketing team should provide a reasonable estimate on the effects of underfunding the marketing program.

Wise marketing professionals keep their supervisors informed during the planning process. This helps supervisors to agree more readily with the marketing program proposal. The management team should not be surprised by the marketing program proposal. Furthermore, because other managers may have a poor understanding of marketing, wise marketing professionals find teachable moments to help other managers understand the purpose of marketing, the underfunding bias, and the importance of building brand strength over the long term.

5.6.7 Refine plans and measures

A good marketing planning process not only leads to the attainment of marketing objectives, it provides a learning format so that marketing planning's effectiveness continually improves over time. Hence, the last step in the process (refine plans and measures) serves as a nexus or prologue for the next planning cycle.

Before embarking on a new planning cycle, the marketing team should closely review its most recent marketing program. Successes that can be leveraged and weaknesses that need correcting need to be identified. Activities that worked well and those that worked poorly should be discussed to discern lessons to learn for improved effectiveness. Discussing these issues and having them held in recent memory will improve planning for the next cycle.

The marketing team should also review its system of metrics. What variables are being measured? Does the marketing team need to improve the way in which a current variable is being measured? Does it need to find a way to measure a new variable?

5.7 Summary

In this chapter, I have emphasized the purpose of marketing—to attract support. Organizations having the greatest need to attract support (many alternatives for potential supporters) rely more heavily on marketing than organizations having less need to attract support (monopolies, for example). Because marketing attracts resources for the organization to attain its objectives, marketing can be held accountable for its effectiveness.

I presented a concept of a theoretically optimum funding level for marketing activities. Funding less than this optimum level is known as underfunding. Funding more than the optimum funding level is known as overfunding. Underfunding and overfunding marketing leads to organizational underperformance. There is a strong underfunding bias in most organizations for several reasons.

Most managers place too much reliance on the short-term tracking of revenues and expenses presented in periodic accounting to inform their decisions. Less effective managers use accounting reports for purposes for which they are not intended. An over-reliance on accounting reports bias's managers thinking (variables used in decision-making) toward an emphasis on expenses and short-term revenue inflows. There are several reasons for this bias.

1. Monetary costs are easy to measure. Returns resulting from those costs are more difficult to measure.

2. The benefits that result from a marketing activity occur later in time (occur sometime after the marketing action has occurred) and may not be captured in the time period of an accounting report.

3. The benefits that result from a marketing activity are dispersed across a time period and may only be partially captured in a current accounting report.

4. Marketing activities can have direct and indirect effects on marketing outcome variables. Indirect effects occur through an intermediate variable (like brand strength) and are unlikely to be accurately measured.

5. Marketing benefits that are not monetarily valued in the short-term are often overlooked. Examples of these variables include brand strength, supporter retention, and supporter lifetime value.

6. The lost benefits of marketing activities that were not funded, but could have acquired support or could have increased the organization's ability to attract support in the future, are not measured.

To help compensate for the underfunding marketing bias, I recommended that an organization use an offsetting adjustment weight. The purpose of the weighted upper-adjustment is to offset the underfunding bias. The use of an effective marketing planning and evaluation system provides for more effective marketing, and learning, that will help improve an organization's ability to fund marketing closer to the optimum level.

I presented a marketing planning process in which marketing objectives are developed to help the organization attain its organizational objectives. Marketing objectives not directly linked to meeting short-term organizational objectives, but which help increase brand strength should also be included. Increasing brand strength will help increase the effectiveness of marketing activities in the future.

Marketing plans are develop to attain specific marketing objectives. An organization's marketing program represents a combination of its marketing plans. Each plan should contain a budget to fund its activities. Each plan should also show when its expenses will be generated. The marketing program should show the summary budget for all the marketing plans as well as a monthly cost projection for funding the marketing program.

6 INCREASING BRAND REMARKABILITY

After studying this chapter you should:

1. Understand the two facets of brand remarkability.

2. Understand how to identify brand object areas for improvement by performing an internal and an external analysis.

3. Understand how to avoid blurring your brand meaning.

1.0 Achieving exceptional excellence individually and in peer comparisons

There are two facets of brand remarkability. The first facet refers to the inherent bundle of brand attributes of the focal brand object. The second facet refers to how the focal brand object compares to its peers (from the perspective of target audiences, of course). We will discuss these two below.

1.1 Your brand

If your organization (using an organization as our brand object example) was the only one in its class (you had no peers or competitors), would your target audiences think that your organization is...

- Excellently managed?

- Doing great work?

- Providing high quality?

- Staffed by highly trained people?

Would your target audiences believe that your organization is managed in an excellent manner? That your organization is exceptionally good at fulfilling its mission or purpose? That your organization makes the maximum use of its resources?

Understanding the answers to these questions is important because they can direct managers' attention to areas needing the most improvement. In analyzing the organization, managers need to make an internal analysis as well as an external analysis. An internal analysis involves managers' assessing the operational excellence of their organizations. An external analysis involves understanding target audiences' perceptions of the excellence of the organization.

1.1.1   Internal analysis

Managers should inform their understanding about what attributes of organizations like theirs are manifestations of excellence in leadership, operations, human research, and mission impact? Trade publications might provide some insights. Also, seeking the assessments of employees may provide useful insights if surveying employee responses can be done anonymously and properly.

Managers should develop a list of factors that serve as indicators of outstanding organizations. My experience talking with managers and business owners is that most will claim that their organization is superior because it provides excellent customer service. Generally, this claim is not supported with evidence. Examples of indicators that might support the claim of excellent customer service might be...

- Less than one percent of customers lodge complaints or service problems annually.

- Our customer retention rate is greater than 90 percent.

- The number of customers we have has grown an average of 15 percent annually over the past five years.

Depending on the nature of the organization, there will be other indicators of excellence. This may involve assessing the quality of human resource management. What is the employee turnover rate? The qualifications of employees (level of training and professionalism)? What is the level of employee satisfaction (morale and enthusiasm)?

With respect to indicators of excellence for nonprofit organizations, one indicator might be the organizations' ability to attract and retain volunteers and donors. The board of directors is an important facet of nonprofit organization management. Excellence indicators with respect to the board of directors might be an assessment of its leadership, board member retention, or board member commitment. Excellence indicators with respect to top administrators might be the board of director's, staff's, volunteers', and donors' confidence in their leadership.

Management professionalism requires that continuous improvement is a mindset that guides managerial attention and emphasis. Managers should look for ways to continually improve the organization, its operations, practices, and procedures. They should have ways of determining how well the organization is performing and the extent to which it is improving.

Next, we will discuss looking outside the organization for help in guiding managerial efforts toward improvements.

1.1.2   External analysis

A very important concept that underlies effective brand management is that it is the perspective of organizations' target audiences that matter most. Unless marketers understand the perspectives of their target audiences (those groups from whom they wish to attract and retain support), they are unlikely to most effective. Hence, marketers should be outward-looking, rather than myopically focused on the internal community of the organization. The organization will have its own perspective. Target audiences will have their own perspectives.

Managers and marketers need to have a realistic understanding of how their organization is perceived by target audiences. Do managers understand their organization's reputation? Do they understand how the community perceives their organization? Is their organization known for something that makes it distinctive?

My experience has been that most organizations do not have a rich understanding of their target audiences' perspectives. Fortunately, there are some exceptional managers that understand their target audiences and usually these managers are quite successful. The difference between informed and uninformed managers appears to be the motivation to clearly understand their target audiences and the motivation to spend time talking regularly with members of their target audiences. There is no substitute for a manager regularly interacting with target audience members.

What else should managers want to know from their target audiences, besides a sense of the organization's reputation? Managers should also want to know what target audiences believe to be substitutes for the organization's products or services. In other words, what are the organization's peer brands? How does the organization compare with its peer brands? What are important brand attributes and how are they ranked in importance? Is the organization, its products or services, perceived to be best among its peer brand set or some other rank?

Although interacting with target audience members is the best source of information that reflects target audience perceptions, other assessment methods can serve important supplemental purposes. For example, collecting data from target audiences through surveys, interviews, or focus groups will provide for a more systematic approach to measure variables and test ideas.

2.0 Sharpening vs. blurring brand meaning

Over time, successful organizations tend to grow. This growth can enable the organization to better achieve its mission. This growth can result in a larger, more complex organization in which managers are placed at a greater distance from target audience members. This growth provides resources for the organization to add additional programs, products, or services. When managers are considering changes to their organizations' product, service, or program mix, they should take into account how those changes will affect their brand (its meaning to target audiences).

As an organization's brand becomes stronger, the organization attracts greater support. The organization acquires more resources as it increases its effectiveness in attracting and retaining support. Managers often view the increased levels of resources as opportunities to expand. In taking advantage of these opportunities, managers may develop brand extensions. Brand extensions refer to offering new products, services, or programs to target groups using the organization's existing brand name.

Managers believe that they can use the brand strength they have generated to more successfully attract support for their new offerings. The effectiveness of brand extensions is dependent upon two key factors. The first factor is the organization's brand strength. The new offering's acceptance by target groups improves as brand strength increases. The second factor is fit. The new offering's acceptance by target groups is influenced by how closely related the new offering is to established brand objects and carry the brand name.

- The success of a brand extension is influence by (1) the original brand's brand strength, and (2) the fit between the original brand and the new offering.

If the two success factors for brand extensions are not met, the success of the new offering will be negatively affected. Furthermore, the launch of the new offering may reduce the brand strength of the original brand if the two key factors are not met.

Launching high quality brand extensions that are a good fit for the original brand leverages the brand strength of the original brand. But, over time, the brand extension reinforces the brand remarkability of the original brand and contributes to the composite brand strength of the organization's mix of offerings. Target audience beliefs about the original brand are confirmed in the brand extension, sharpening the brand meaning of the original and extended brands.

When the key success factors are met, but the extended brand has a lower quality that the original brand, the extended brand may enjoy some initial unwarranted support because of the brand strength effect of the original brand. However, over time, the support for the extended brand will ebb. Of greater concern is the possibility that the lower-quality extended brand will reduce the brand remarkability of the original brand.

2.1 Managing new offerings when key success factors are not met

When the two success factors are not met, it is advisable not to use a brand extension strategy for the new offering. Instead, a new brand identity can be developed for the new offering, foregoing an attempt to take advantage of the brand strength of the original brand. If the original brand has low brand strength, there is little benefit for the new offering of associating it with the original brand. If the new offering is a poor fit with the original brand, then the association may weaken the original brand.

There are two dimensions of fit between the original brand and the new offering: comparative quality and comparative function. If the new offering's quality is substantially greater than or less than the original brand, there is a poor fit between the two. If the purpose or function of the new offering is substantially different from the original brand, there is a poor fit between the two. We will next examine the implications of these two sources of poor fit.

2.1.1 Substantially different quality

Ritz-Carlton hotels are high quality hotels in the luxury category. The high priced accommodations are positioned to attract affluent travelers who expect luxury and a high level of service. What if the managers at Ritz wanted to develop a chain of budget motels for price sensitive family vacationers? If they gave the new budget chain the Ritz-Carlton brand name, the budget chain would have instant brand recognition, but at a cost of significant erosion of brand strength of the original brand. Instead Ritz's managers will probably give the new chain its own brand identity (Perhaps the Come & Go Motel?) and not promote the fact that the two hotel chains are owned by the same parent company.

Hotel corporations that have expanded into multiple chains that are configured to attract different categories of guests, and, therefore, have different quality levels, often give the chains different brand names. For example, the Ritz-Carlton is now owned by Marriott International, which owns several hotel chains in a variety of categories.

Car companies employ a similar brand strategy. Toyota Motor Corporation has developed the Toyota car brand into a strong brand. The key brand attributes of the Toyota brand are a very reliable vehicle, moderately priced, with a long operational life. Toyota has expanded its offerings from the A1 and G1 passenger cars in 1935 to an array of vehicles that include cars, trucks, and SUVs.

In 1989, Toyota wanted to expand its offerings into the luxury or premium car market. Rather than give the new car model the Toyota brand name, Toyota give it the brand name Lexus. This was a way for Toyota to disassociate the new premium car brand from its original brand name. Toyota is a brand for the general market, for the average person. Lexus is a brand for the affluent person seeking to demonstrate prestige.

The examples discussed show that when a new offering is substantially different from target audiences' comprehensions of the brand, it may be advisable to launch the new offering under its own brand name. In our examples, had Ritz and Toyota decided to launch their new offerings as brand extensions (the new offering uses the original brand name), the outcome may have been disappointing. In the case in which the new offering has significantly higher quality than the original brand (Lexus vs. Toyota), the new brand's premium image may be reduced to the average associated with the main brand. In the case in which the new offering has significantly lower quality than the original brand (Come & Go Motel vs. Ritz), the association would reduce the brand strength of Ritz (by reducing Ritz's brand remarkability).

Next, we will discuss another category of poor fit. That is, poor fit exists when the new offering is functionally different (or serves a different purpose) from the original brand.

2.1.2 Substantially different function

Let of use a fictitious service business as an example. We will call it Reliant Legal Services (RLS). Imagine that Reliant has two attorneys who usually work on family law issues. Any additional offerings that RLS might offer that are related to legal services would serve as examples of new offerings having similar functions. Some examples are listed in Table 1.

In Table 1, three examples of new offerings that are functionally-related to the core service of the original brand are provided. The first example, criminal defense services, is a variant of the original brand's parent category, in-person legal services to individuals. RLS currently practices family law. The parent service category is legal services. Offering criminal defense legal services would be functionally similar. Therefore, assuming RLS is a strong brand, adding criminal defense services as brand extension would be an appropriate brand strategy for the new offering.

Table 1. RLS Functionally Similar Brand Extensions

Nature of extension	Example
A variant of the original brand's parent category	Criminal defense
Different form of original brand's service	Do-it-yourself will kits
Companion service	Investigative services

In the second extension example in Table 1, RLS wants to offer do-it-yourself will kits. For a fixed fee, customers could purchase and download an online template which would help customers prepare their own wills. This is an example of a new offering which is a different form (self-service, online) from the original brand's service (personal service, in person). Because of the functional similarities between the original brand and the new offering, a brand extension strategy would still be appropriate (assuming RLS is a strong brand). The extension (online do-it-yourself will kits) and the original offering of RLS are both legal services.

In the third extension example in Table 1, the new offering (investigative services) is a type of companion service of the original brand's service. That is, sometimes legal practices need to hire an investigator to gather facts and information for their clients that require special investigative skill sets. RLS may have contracted with a private investigator when it needed these services in the past. However, RLS may believe it can offer its own investigative services to its legal clients as well as to other law firms. Because of the functional linkage between legal and investigative services, RLS would offer the investigative services as a brand extension using its original brand name.

When the new offering is not functionally similar to that of the original brand, it may be advisable to provide the new offering with its own brand identity. In our next example, we will use a common consumer product, laundry bleach. The strongest brand in this category is Clorox bleach. The primary brand attributes of Clorox laundry bleach are that it is a strong (1) disinfectant, (2) stain remover, and (3) brightener of white fabrics. As a successful brand, Clorox's brand strength enabled it to expand, which lead to new product offerings. Examples are provided in Table 2.

Table 2. Clorox Brand Extensions

Product type	*Brand names*
Laundry aids	Clorox Stain Fighter Clorox Stain Remover and Color Booster Clorox Oxi Magic Clorox Bleach Stain Remover for Whites
Household cleaners	Clorox Bleach Gel Clorox Fraganzia Multi-Purpose Cleaner Clorox Blue Automatic Toilet Bowl Cleaner Clorox Glass Wipes Formula 409 Green Works natural cleaners

	Pine-Sol, Tilex, and S.O.S. cleaning products
Non-household disinfectants	Clorox Disinfecting Wipes On The Go
Other household products	Clorox Freshcare Towels Clorox Cleaning Tools Kingsford charcoal Glad trash bags Liquid-Plummer drain cleaner
Walter filtration systems	Brita water filter systems & products
Natural cosmetics and personal care products	Burt's Bees
Pet care (cats and dogs)	Clorox Urine Remover Fresh Step, Scoop Away , and Ever Clean cat litters
Food products	Hidden Valley brand dressings and spreads Kitchen Bouquet, KC Masterpiece, and Soy Vay sauces

The Clorox Company has been careful to limit its brand extensions (launching new products using the Clorox brand name) to products that are a good fit. Note that the products that have the Clorox brand name have a functional relationship to cleaning, stain removing, disinfecting, or bleaching.

While Table 2 does not list all of Clorox products, it presents the various categories of products Clorox has added to its product mix. Most of the products listed in Table 2 that do not carry the Clorox brand name were strong brands that were acquired by the Clorox Company. Clorox added a line of natural cleaning products to its product mix, Green Works, to appeal to environmentally-conscious consumers and to promote its corporate social responsibility.

Note the Clorox Company's brand strategy. It develops new products that are related to its original brand's key attributes. This maintains fit between extended brands with the original brand.

Sometimes Clorox acquires or licenses other company's strong brands.

Since these acquired brands are already strong, Clorox markets those products without associating them with the Clorox brand name. Sometimes the acquired brands are related to Clorox's key brand attributes (e.g., Formula 409, Pine-Sol). Sometimes the acquired brands are unrelated to Clorox's key products (e.g., Brita, Liquid-Plummer, Fresh Step, Hidden Valley).

In the case in which Clorox wanted to launch a new line of products to be contrasted and differentiated from its original brand attributes (e.g., Green Works), Clorox chose not to use a brand extension strategy. Instead, it launched the new line of products a new brand name--Green Works.

3.0 Brand remarkability and brand attribute analysis

Clorox's success in maintaining its brand strength while expanding its product mix was dependent upon its managers understanding how its brand object was comprehended by its customers. Clorox meant clean. It meant brightening whites. It meant disinfecting. Clorox was exceptional with respect to this three-attribute combination. That is, Clorox was a strong fabric whitener. It was a strong disinfectant. It was a strong cleaning agent.

Hence, it is the (1) combination of attributes, and (2) comparative performance of attributes that differentiates a brand from its peers.

- Target audiences prefer brands that are exceptionally strong on the attributes they consider most important.

3.1 Assess the value of attributes

For an organization to effectively understand how target audiences perceive its brand attributes and its peer brands' attributes, market research can be useful. While there is no substitute for managers' personal involvement with target audiences, this is not always sufficient or practical.

It is important to understand that limiting marketing research to one's own brand is insufficient to inform a manager about a target audience's perception of the brand. This is because target audiences view a brand in the context of its peers. Hence, a manager must also understand how the brand it perceived in this context.

One theoretical approach to model our understanding of brand attributes is derived from Herzberg's two-factor theory. (The interested reader is referred to http://en.wikipedia.org/wiki/Two-factor_theory for a more detailed explanation.) Applying the two-factor theory in the context of brand attributes, our target audience perceives each of the brand attribute to either be a motivation attribute or a hygiene attribute. A **motivation attribute** is a brand attribute that influences target audience preference. That is, the presence of this motivation attribute is a positive influence on target audience preference. **Hygiene attributes** are those brand attribute that do not motivate preference, but if they were absent from the brand object, would make the brand appear deficient, substandard, and unsatisfactory.

The presence of motivation attributes has a positive influence on target audience preference. The absence of hygiene factors has a negative influence on preference. Using hotels as an example, there are several attributes related to this brand object which are presented in Table 3.

Table 3. Typical Hotel Brand Attributes

Hotel reputation & rating	Free cable TV	Airport transportation
Price	Room size	Check in and check out speed
Free parking	Hotel appearance & decoration	Laundry service
Free breakfast	Cleanliness	Free Wi-Fi
Free local calls	Friendliness of staff	Room service
Self-service laundry	Attentiveness of staff	Free newspapers

- The presence of motivation attributes has a positive influence on target audience preference.
- The absence of hygiene factors has a negative influence on preference.

Table 3 presents some examples of hotel attributes of varying important to hotel guests. Determining which attributes are important to guests requires a specification of guest type. There are different types of guests with different attribute preferences. You have business travelers, tourist groups, family vacationers, leisure travelers, event attenders, and so forth. For purposes of this example, let us assume our target audience is the family vacationer on a budget.

In Table 4 each attribute is designated as either a motivation or as hygiene attribute.

Table 4. Hotel Brand Attribute Categories And Rankings

	Attribute type	*Ranking*
Hotel reputation & rating	Motivation	3
Low Price	Motivation	1
Free parking	Hygiene	2
Free breakfast	Motivation	2
Free local calls	Hygiene	7
Self-service laundry	Motivation	4
Free cable TV	Hygiene	6
Room size	Motivation	5
Hotel appearance & decoration	Motivation	6
Cleanliness	Hygiene	1
Friendliness of staff	Motivation	7
Attentiveness of staff	Hygiene	8
Airport transportation	Not relevant	
Check in and check out speed	Hygiene	9
Laundry service	Hygiene	5
Free Wi-Fi	Hygiene	3
Room service	Not relevant	

Free newspapers	Not relevant	
Bed & pillow comfort	Hygiene	4

In practice, we would determine the type of attribute from our marketing research. Furthermore, the results of our research will us to rank each attribute with respect to its importance to members of the target audience. Note that we discovered a couple of attributes which held little importance to members of our target audience.

In Table 4, for our budget-sensitive family travelers, some hotel attributes are motivation factors, some are hygiene factors, and some are not relevant (they do not matter to this audience). Note that some attributes are more important than others. The most important motivation factor is price. Our target audience is traveling on a budget and price is important. The availability of a free breakfast is the second most important motivation factor because our family travelers perceive the free breakfast to be an important feature that adds value to their hotel experience.

Keep in mind that family travelers are not only interested in finding a hotel with the lowest price. It is the combination of motivation and hygiene factors that is important. The target audience will most prefer the hotel with the attribute ranking that is most congruent with their own hotel attribute preferences. For the hotel that wants to be the strongest brand for family travelers on a budget, it needs to have the same attribute emphasis that appeals to this target audience.

Next, we will discuss some methods for gathering information from target audiences to inform our understanding of their perceptions of our brand and its peers. Essentially, keep in mind the guiding process for conducting a remarkability analysis.

Step 1   Discover which brand object attributes are preferred by the target audience.

Step 2   Assess how your brand is perceived by the target audience with respect to its defining attributes.

Step 3   Assess how peer brands are perceived by the target audience with respect to their defining attributes.

Step 4   Compare the target brand's attribute profile with its peers.

Step 5   Determine which target brand attributes should be improved upon.

Obviously, completing steps 1-3 will require gathering accurate information and insights from the target audience. We will discuss some of the methods for gathering information from a target audience below.

3.1.1 Qualitative methods

Qualitative information gathering methods involve talking with or observing members of the target audience. Qualitative methods typically involve gathering information from a relatively small number of individuals from the target audience. Marketers spend more time with each target audience member interviewing them, for example, than they would using quantitative methods (like survey research[1]).

In qualitative research, marketers are interested in gathering insights and developing a richer understanding of the target audience's perspective. Target audience members who participate in qualitative research are en-

---

[1] Although one could argue that open-ended survey questions collect qualitative data, for brevity we will not make this distinction.

BRAND MANAGEMENT

couraged to describe their perspectives, opinions, preferences, and experiences. Some of the more regularly used qualitative methods are discussed next.

3.1.1.1 Focus groups

Eight to 12 members of the target audience are recruited to participate in a discussion related to the brand. A marketer will moderate the small group discussion. The focus group discussion typically lasts between 60 and 90 minutes. Sometimes the discussion is audio/video recorded.

The justification for using focus groups is that the small group interactions will stimulate ideas and discussions that might not surface during separate individual interviews. There is a small group communication dynamic that may percolate insights into the discussion. A skilled and experienced moderator is important to attaining successful focus group outcomes.

Methods for recruiting focus group participants vary, depending on the target audience profile. Sometimes, for example, newspaper ads are purchased to recruit focus group participants. Sometimes, focus group participants are paid or given other compensation for their involvement. Individuals often enjoy the experience of participating in a focus group because of the interest and attention given to their opinions and ideas.

Usually, marketers conduct multiple focus groups, not just a single focus group. The general rule for the number of needed focus groups is that you continue to conduct focus groups until no new insights are retrieved. In practice, four to eight focus groups are usually sufficient to retrieve the insights that may be gleaned from this type of qualitative research.

3.1.1.2 Personal interviews

When people communicate face-to-face, much more information is communicated between them than in other methods of gathering information. There are other advantages as well. If the interviewee (the person being interviewed) does not quite understand the question being asked, she can ask the interviewer to clarify the question. The personal interview format also allows the interviewer opportunities to explore in greater depth topics that may arise during the interview.

Interviewees must be recruited from the target audience. The marketing professional must also decide how many people to interview. For example, the marketer may begin with a base number of 25 interviewees. After 25 interviews the marketer can determine how much similarity exists among the responses from the interviews. If the interview data are converging into a set of common themes, ideas, and responses; then 25 interviews may be sufficient. However, if the interview data are still producing new insights and ideas, then more interviews may be useful.

If members of the target audience are dispersed geographically, then telephone interviews may be a good alternative. I once conducted a series of telephone interviews using the Internet. I used Skype to conduct the phone call and used an application called Amolto to record the Skype interviews. The audio recordings were transcribed into text files by a research assistant. A research colleague analyzed and interpreted the transcribed text data.

3.1.1.3 Expert opinions

Interviewing experts may provide useful insights. An expert is someone who is knowledgeable about the brand, brand object, peer brands, or target audience. Experts, if available, can provide helpful insights. Managers within an organization often have their perspectives influenced from the organizational context and culture. Experts' perspectives do not have the same organizational influence, potentially giving them the ability to have helpful insights.

3.1.1.4 Regular interaction with target audiences

Whichever data collection methods are used, they should be complemented with regular managerial interaction with members of target audiences. There really is no substitute for managers personally interacting with target audience members. Managers can better understand target audience perspectives through regular interactions and involvement. Engaged managers can also make better use of data because their interpretations of the data are more realistic. Engaged managers can also better discern which findings from the data analysis are useful and which are not.

3.1.2 Quantitative methods

Qualitative methods allow target audience responses to remain in their natural state. For example, discourse data remains text. Quantitative methods are designed so that target audience responses produce numeric data. There are advantages to each type of research method.

Qualitative methods are useful when exploring in an in-depth manner ideas and perspectives of a relatively small number of target audience members. The purpose of qualitative methods is to help managers understand the perspectives of the target audience. When managers believe they have arrived at a realistic understanding of their target audiences, they can test this understanding using quantitative methods on much larger numbers of audience members.

For example, it managers believe they have learned the top motivation and hygiene attributes from their focus group research, they can test this belief by conducting survey research using a representative sample of the target audience. If managers are considering important decisions based on qualitative research findings, they would be prudent to confirm the findings in a quantitative research study first.

Since the most common type of data collection method for quantitative research is survey research, I will assume the reader will also use survey research. There are different pathways for presenting survey questions to a representative sample of the target audience. Typically, marketers use mail (post) surveys, online surveys, or telephone surveys. Online surveys are becoming more popular because of their low cost when an appropriate sample is available.

Next, we will discuss the most common ways of assessing the differential importance of brand attributes. One of the assumptions of assessing attribute importance using surveys is that the attributes that matter to the target audience are known to managers and are accounted for in the survey. One of the key purposes of qualitative research is to develop a target audience's list of relevant brand attributes, which are subsequently tested and analyzed in quantitative research.

3.1.2.1 Ranking by ordinal choice

Getting survey participants to rank order brand attributes can be particularly insightful. It places target audience members into a task in which they have to decide which attributes are more important and which are less important. (See Table 5.)

In Table 5, an example is presented in which survey participants are given a ranking task. (Obviously it is important that you sample of survey participants is representative of the target audience.) Each survey participant will rank the hotel motivation attributes according to each's perceived importance in selecting a hotel. The rank order data generated from the survey may be averaged. For example, the average rank score for each attribute can be calculated.

Table 5. Hotel Brand Motivation Attribute Ranking Example

Directions to survey participants: Below is a list of five common hotel features. Rank each according to its importance to you in selecting a hotel. Place a 1 for the feature that is most important to you. Place a 5 for the feature that is least important to you.	
Hotel feature	*Ranking*
Hotel reputation & rating	
Low Price	
Room size	
Free breakfast	
Hotel appearance & decor	

In Table 6, the ranking averages from a fictitious sample of survey participants are presented. The hotel motivation attributes listed in Table 5 are reordered in Table 6 according to their averages. Interpret the findings with care. We can say with confidence that our target audience believes that a low price is the most important hotel motivation attribute. We can conclude that a low price and a free breakfast are more important than the hotel's reputation and rating and the hotel's appearance and decoration.

Table 6. Hotel Attribute Ranking Averages

Hotel feature	*Ave Score*
Low Price	1.5
Free breakfast	2.1
Room size	3.7
Hotel reputation & rating	3.8
Hotel appearance & decoration	4.2

You cannot have as much confidence in your interpretations of items that were ranked near the middle of the list. For example, survey respondents are less certain of the middle-ranked preferences. They more clearly understand what attributes that they like most and like least. Therefore, you cannot be confident that room size is really more important than hotel reputation and rating.

The ranking procedure can be particularly useful when managers want to better understand audience preferences between alternative attributes. As the number of attributes increases, the ranking task requires more effort from survey participants. It is best to keep the attribute list below 15 if possible.

When interpreting attribute data, it is important to remember that it is the combination of attributes and the way in which the combination is ranked that matters. In Table 6, we see that the hotel's appearance and decoration attribute is ranked last. This does not mean that this attribute is not important to the target audience. It simply means that the attribute is less important than a free breakfast, for example, in influencing hotel preference. As the number of attributes that are listed grows, you can become more confident that the lowest ranked attributes have comparatively less influence on audience member preference. When having a set of only five attributes, however, it would be imprudent to assume that the lowest ranked attribute does not matter to audience members.

3.1.2.2 Ranking by mean rating scores

Some researchers prefer to have survey respondents consider the attributes independently rather than comparatively. Each attribute is rated independently instead of ranked comparatively. In this case, the relative importance of each attribute is assessed without asking the survey respondent to compare the perceived importance of one attribute with another attribute.

In Table 7, I have provided a simple example of a set of survey questions that would be used to acquire brand attribute rating (instead of ranking) data from a target audience sample. Survey respondents are asked to indicate their level of agreement with statements for each brand attribute. Think of each brand attribute statement as a variable. Each survey participant will provide a number (from 1 to 5) for each variable. All the numbers for each variable are combined, summed, and averaged for interpretation.

Table 7. Hotel Hygiene Attribute Rating Example

Directions to survey participants:
Circle the one answer that best reflects your level of agreement with each of the following statements.

I will only stay in a hotel room that was is clean.				
Strongly disagree 1	Disagree 2	Neither agree or disagree 3	Agree 4	Strongly agree 5
I will only stay in a hotel that has a self-service laundry.				
Strongly disagree 1	Disagree 2	Neither agree or disagree 3	Agree 4	Strongly agree 5
I will only stay in a hotel that has free parking.				
Strongly disagree 1	Disagree 2	Neither agree or disagree 3	Agree 4	Strongly agree 5
I will only stay in a hotel that has free Wi-Fi.				
Strongly disagree 1	Disagree 2	Neither agree or disagree 3	Agree 4	Strongly agree 5
I will only stay in a hotel that has a comfortable bed and pillows.				
Strongly disagree 1	Disagree 2	Neither agree or disagree 3	Agree 4	Strongly agree 5

Survey respondent scores are averaged like they were with the rank order data. Table 8 provides an example of hotel hygiene average rating scores. The attributes are listed in descending order by importance. Cleanliness is most important. Free parking is least important.

Table 8. Hotel Attribute Rating Averages

Hotel feature	Ave Score
Cleanliness	4.1
Free Wi-Fi	3.9
Comfortable bed & pillows	3.4
Self-service laundry	3.1
Free parking	2.7

Care should be taken when interpreting the findings. It is reasonable to conclude from the data averages presented in Table 8 that survey participants believe that hotel cleanliness is more important than the availability of free parking. It is reasonable to conclude that cleanliness and free Wi-Fi are more important than a self-service laundry and free parking. It is more difficult to make conclusions about attributes whose scores are quite close, especially when using small sample sizes. For example, the average rating for cleanliness is 0.2 points higher than for free Wi-Fi. Hence, both cleanliness and free Wi-Fi are important even though cleanliness may be *slightly* more important.

Because there are relatively few attributes (five) in our example, care should be taken when making decisions about the brand attributes. For example, free parking is the least important hygiene attribute. This does not necessarily mean that the hotel that currently offers free parking can begin to charge for parking and experience no consequences. It does mean, however, that target audience members generally find hotel cleanliness to be a more important hotel attribute than free parking.

3.1.2.3 Advanced statistical procedures (conjoint analysis)

The ranking procedures described in the prior sections are relatively simple procedures that are easy to analyze. The procedures are also robust and sound. The usefulness of any procedure is only as good as the quality of the sample and questionnaire permit. If the sample is not representative of the target audience or the survey questions do not include the relevant attributes, the findings produced will be invalid regardless of how the data are analyzed.

Having made this important point, however, I would be remiss if I did not mention to the reader that there are some more sophisticated techniques for assessing attribute importance. A detailed discussion of these techniques is beyond the scope of this chapter.

Conjoint analysis is a popular type of advanced technique used to evaluate the comparative importance of brand attributes. As a basic explanation of conjoint analysis, the brand attributes are first paired. For example, if there were three brand attributes, we would have three pairs (1+2, 1+3, 2+3). Survey respondents are given a task in which they have to indicate a preference for one pair of attributes over another pair of attributes. The logic behind conjoint analysis is that survey participants are forced to make trade-offs among attributes, thereby revealing the relative importance of the attributes. Assuming that the sample is representative of the target audience and that a relatively small set of attributes is relevant to the target audience, conjoint analysis is a very useful technique.

Conjoint analysis becomes difficult to implement as the number of attributes increases. For example, if the number of attributes increases from three attributes to 15 attributes, the number of attribute pairs increases from three to 105.[2] Few survey participants would have the patience to complete such a time consuming survey.

3.1.3 Secondary research

The examples of data collection thus far are considered to be primary research. Marketers may find some secondary research available that might be useful. Secondary research or secondary data refers to information or data that was collected for some other purpose, but is available to the marketer for their own subsequent analysis. For example, if a major hotel chain surveyed its guests to determine which hotel features they believed to be most important, and if the hotel chain is willing to let your organization

---

[2] The interested reader who wants to know how to calculate the number of attribute pairs may refer to http://math.stackexchange.com/questions/102005/formula-for-counting-pairs-in-a-set

have access to its data, then you might be able to develop some insights from this information. For the hotel chain, the data was generated from primary research. For your organization, the data represents secondary data and your analysis of the secondary data represents secondary research.

It is usually best for an organization to perform its own research. However, a search through secondary data sources might be worth the effort if information about an organization's target audiences or peer brands can be identified. Secondary research, if available, could be from either public or private sources. Public sources refer to research that was funded by the government and is stored in a government branch or academic facility. Private sources refer to research that was funded by a nonprofit or commercial organization and either distributed to members (members of industry trade associations, for example) or sold by market research firms.

3.2 Construct comparison tables

Once the appropriate information has been obtained on the target audience's perceptions of your brand attributes and those of your close peers, it is helpful to construct a comparison table to facilitate your analysis. We will use Table 9 for an example using the hotel motivation attribute results presented previously.

Table 9. Comparison of Motivation Attributes*

Attribute	Our hotel	Peer brand A	Peer brand B
Low price	7	10	5
Free breakfast	8	3	9
Room size	8	4	7
Hotel reputation	8	6	7
Hotel appearance	6	4	7

Note: Attributes are rated on a 1-10 scale. 1 is lowest score; 10 is highest score.

In Table 9, the left column contains the hotel motivation attributes in descending order of importance to the target audience. All of the attributes are important, but the low price is the most important attribute. Your hotel and your two key competitors (peer brand A and peer brand B) complete the remaining columns. For each motivation attribute ratings from target audience data are provided for the three hotels being compared. The target audience rated each hotel according to how strong it is with respect to the five motivation attributes. The rating scale ranged from 1 to 10. The number one was the lowest score; the number 10 was the highest score.

The target audience's brand (hotel) preference is derived from a hotel's performance on the *bundle* of attributes rather than on any single attribute. However, the attributes are weighted differently according to how important they are perceived by the target audience. After examining the information in Table 9, we can conclude that our hotel is in a relatively strong competitive position. Peer brand A has the lowest price, which is probably the core message in its advertising. Peer brand A, however, rates relatively low on the remaining attributes. Our hotel is priced lower than peer brand B and is perceived slightly stronger than peer brand B on two of the four remaining attributes (room size and hotel reputation), and weaker than peer brand B on two of the four remaining attributes (free breakfast and hotel appearance).

With respect to what our hotel can do to make itself more remarkable, we can take actions to increase our score on any of the five motivation brand attributes. It is probably difficult and unappealing for us to lower our price further. This might involve cost cutting measures that would lower other attribute scores. Our competitive strategy with peer brand A is not to compete with it for the lowest price, but to position ourselves as being a better value than peer brand A. If you stay at Hotel A, you might pay a low price, but you're staying in a cheap hotel. If you stay in our hotel, you might pay a little more than if you stayed in Hotel A, but you get a lot more value in return—you will have a much better hotel experience.

In competing with peer brand B (Hotel B), we charge a little less, which is good because this is the most important attribute for our target audience. However, Hotel B has a better breakfast than we offer at our hotel and Hotel B has a better appearance. The room size is a relatively fixed attribute that is costly to change. Therefore, if Hotel B increases its room size to compete with us it will probably have to increase price which would increase a lower ranked attribute but decrease a higher ranked attribute (an unlikely choice for Hotel B to make). The same logic applies to the hotel appearance attribute. Our hotel performs a bit less on appearance than Hotel B, but improving the appearance would increase our cost and, therefore, we might have to raise our price. Hence, we would want to avoid improving a less important attribute while worsening a more important attribute.

It would seem that the most sensible tactic would be to improve the quality of our breakfast. This would cause us to incur a cost, but the cost is comparatively small considering the scale of our business and should not require a price increase. If we could improve the breakfast sufficiently to obtain an audience rating a 10, this would give us additional separation (differentiation) from Hotel A and Hotel B.

Next, we will evaluate the hotel hygiene attributes in Table 10. Recall that hygiene attributes are those attributes that the target audience expects the hotel to offer as a standard for this class of hotel. A hotel which is deficient on a hygiene attribute is perceived to be substandard on that attribute, which can negatively influence customer preference for a hotel brand. Some hygiene attributes are more important than others and a hotel can vary with respect to how bad or substandard it is with respect to a hygiene attribute. Hence, the degree to which insufficient performance on a hygiene attribute negatively influences hotel brand preference is related to how important the hygiene attribute is perceived and how poorly the hotel performs on that hygiene attribute.

Table 10. Comparison of Hygiene Attributes*

Attribute	Our hotel	Peer brand A	Peer brand B
Cleanliness	8	5	8
Free Wi-Fi	4	6	7
Comfortable bed & pillows	7	3	7
Self-service laundry	7	7	3
Free parking	10	10	10

Note: Attributes are rated on a 1-10 scale. 1 is lowest score; 10 is highest score.

From examining target audience evaluations of our hotel and our peer brands (our closest competitors), it appears that we generally meet our target audience standards on these hygiene attributes. It appears, however, that we might have a problem with respect to our target audience's perception of our Wi-Fi. In the economy class of hotels Wi-Fi is typically offered to guests free of charge. (Luxury hotels are known to charge a premium for an internet connection.) However, while guests in our category of hotel view free Wi-Fi as a standard feature, they also expect the free Wi-Fi to have an acceptable performance level.

Like other hotels, we contract with a local internet service provider for our internet connectivity. We generally contract for the lowest priced service available to hotels. As a consequence, we have a somewhat restricted service. Our guests' Wi-Fi connection is adequate enough for web page viewing and checking email, but it is insufficient for downloading large files. In the evenings, when most of our guests are in their rooms, the Wi-Fi traffic is congested and web pages download quite slowly.

In deciding our options for dealing with the substandard performance on our Wi-Fi service, we have several alternatives. Taking into account our need to improve our Wi-Fi service while not substantially increasing our operational costs, we believe the following to the Wi-Fi service decisions will improve our audience rating on this hygiene attribute from a four to a more respectable seven.

1. Contract for a moderate level of internet connectivity from our broadband provider. This will have better performance than the economy package we currently use, but not dramatically increase our costs.

2. We will make our guests aware that if they desire premium level Wi-Fi speeds, they can individually purchase a daily account from our internet service provider. Hence, for guests who demand premium internet connectivity, and they are not too price sensitive, they can purchase high speed Wi-Fi separately from our internet service provider.

3. We will instruct our internet service provider to block certain file types and internet sites from our free Wi-Fi service so that guests cannot hoard bandwidth from other guests by downloading or streaming large files. This will prevent a few guests from sharply slowing the connection speed for the other guests.

Returning to our examination of Table 10, we note that Hotel B rates poorly on its self-service laundry. Our target audience, family travelers on a budget, likes having the option of washing their clothes in a self-service laundry. Hotels that have this attribute often have a room available to guests in which coin-operated washing machines and clothes dryers are placed. For a hotel to attain a low rating on this attribute it might not offer a self-service laundry or, if it does offer a self-service laundry, guests may find the laundry service to be inadequate. There are many reasons why a self-service laundry could be inadequate. There may be too few machines available to guests, the prices may be too high, the laundry room may in a state of disrepair, and so forth. The fact that Hotel B is substandard on this attribute provides our hotel with an opportunity to differentiate itself.

With respect to Hotel A (from Table 10), we note that it is substandard on cleanliness (the most important hygiene attribute) and having comfortable beds and pillows. Hence, we can further emphasize the poor value that accompanies the low price for Hotel A in our target audience communications.

4.0 Make necessary improvements in remarkability

By using our brand attribute analysis as described in the previous section, we have a process for identifying brand attributes that are important to our target audience. We have a process for determining the priority our target audience gives to each attribute, allowing us to establish a ranking or weighting of attributes with respect to their perceived importance. Our process enables us to evaluate how our target audience perceives our brand and our peer brands with respect to the key brand attributes. Hence, we have a method of informing our decisions that emphasize attributes most likely to attract and retain support from our target audience.

Availing ourselves of the brand attribute analysis process, we can determine if our brand is under-performing on an important attribute. We can determine if we can further distinguish our brand on other attributes. There is an underlying assumption, however. We assume that we will *have the ability* to influence changes in our organization or our brand objects. In our hotel example, we believed we could improve our brand remarkability by improving the quality of our breakfast and the quality of our Wi-Fi service. We took into account the practicality of potential changes and the potential impact of those changes on improving our ability to attract and retain our guests.

Our described attribute analysis process is consistent with a continuous improvement management program. This refers to a managerial mindset that believes it is important for regularly finding ways to improve the organization and its offerings. Whereas the typical management improvement perspective emphasizes increasing operational efficiency and lowering operational costs, our marketing perspective emphasizes improving the organization's ability to attract and retain its target audience, those people from whom it depends for its continued success.

We would advise traditionally-oriented managers who continually look for ways to lower costs to include in their decision process the impact of their changes on the organization's brand attributes. Lowering costs while unknowingly lowering the brand strength of the organization seems like an ill-conceived trade-off. Unfortunately, managers who fail to take into account the effect of their decisions on brand strength may be weakening the organization's ability to attract and retain support for the benefit of short-term cost reductions.

5.0 Adjust messaging to reflect emphasis on more important attributes

In our description of the brand attribute analysis process for improving brand remarkability, we looked for ways in which we could improve certain attributes that could provide a competitive advantage to the organization. By better understanding how our brand's bundle of attributes distinguishes it from its peers, the positioning of our brand to our target audiences is made more clearly. In Table 9, we discovered that our hotel can be promoted favorably in comparison to Hotel A as a better value. Although Hotel A offers guests a lower price, Hotel A underperforms on the remaining important motivation attributes. Hence, our message could be that our hotel is a better value than Hotel A. *For a slightly higher price, you get a lot better experience.*

In competing with Hotel B, we would also promote ourselves to the target audience as a better value. *For a lower price than Hotel B charges, you get just a good an experience while staying at our hotel—making us a better value.* We recommended improving the quality of our breakfast. If we are able to surpass the quality of Hotel B's breakfast, we could argue in our advertisements that if you stay at our hotel instead of Hotel B, you'll get a better experience and also pay a lower price. From our marketing research, we know that these attributes are important to our target audience.

As you can see, then, understanding which of your brand attributes to improve and emphasize, you are better able to effectively differentiate yourself from your peer brands. Furthermore, your informed understanding of your brand's attribute bundle informs your communications strategy.

7 INCREASING BRAND FAMILIARITY

After studying this chapter you should:

1. Understand the important role of brand familiarity in establishing brand strength.

2. Understand the importance of continually improving brand re-markability.

3. Understand that communications about the brand must be truthful and believable.

4. Understand how audience brand perceptions are determined.

5. Understand the steps in managing media relations.

6. Understand the steps in managing communications during a crisis.

7. Understand the steps in developing an annual communications plan.

1.0 Introduction

The overarching strategic marketing goal that drives the need to com-municate to target audiences is increasing brand strength. Communicating with target audiences is the essential element of increasing brand familiarity. The more you communicate with your target audiences, the more they will know about your brand object, and the more your brand familiarity will in-crease.

Furthermore, even though brand remarkability is a different brand strength dimension than brand familiarity, there exists interdependency between them. Recall that brand remarkability is entirely determined by the perceptions of target audiences. If target audiences are unfamiliar with your brand object then you have little or no brand remarkability--regardless of how good your brand object actually is. This is because target audiences have insufficient knowledge about your brand object to make an assessment.

- If brand familiarity is very low, then brand remarkability cannot be determined. Hence, brand strength will also be very low.

Brand familiarity is a prime mover of brand strength. However, as target audiences become more familiar with the brand object, they can begin to develop stronger perceptions (beliefs and opinions) about the brand object and how it compares to its peers. As brand familiarity increases, brand remarkability's influence on brand strength grows. For example, a company offers a new product that would be perceived to be remarkable if consumers knew about the product. Over time, as consumers become more familiar with the product, brand remarkability increases as does brand strength.

Another outcome can occur, of course, if the evolving brand remarkability is low. For example, using a fictitious oil company, image that the company has a history of major accidents and has been found to be negligent, in effect, causing the accidents that caused injury and harm. The more people know about the oil company (brand familiarity increases), the more they will view the oil company as being quite unremarkable, the more brand attitudes toward the oil company will be strongly negative. Hence, high brand familiarity may amplify the effects of an unfavorable set of brand attributes, reducing brand strength.

- Communications about the brand object need to be truthful and believable.

- Major brand attribute weaknesses need to be corrected before building brand familiarity.

It is quite important for managers to realize that they only partly control brand familiarity. People receive information from many different sources. The messages sent by an organization to its target audiences represent only one source of information about the brand object.

- Target audience perceptions are informed by their experiences and by the information they receive.

Put simply, target audiences develop their perceptions about a brand based on information they receive about the brand object (and its peers) and their personal experiences with the brand object (and its peers). Managers, then, have a great deal of control with respect to the information the organization sends to its target audiences. Managers have a good deal of control with respect to target audiences' personal experiences with the brand. Managers have very little control with respect to other sources of information about the brand object (and its peers) and about audience experiences with peer brands.

1.1 Information you can control

Generally there are two categories of communications that are under the control of managers. They are (1) messages sent directly from someone in the organization to target audience members and (2) messages the organization pays an intermediary to send to target audience members.

One concept presented earlier in this book is that there is no better way to understand an organization's target audiences than for managers to interact and engage with target audience members. This concept also applies with respect to communication. There is no better way for the organization to communicate with its target audience than personal contact between members of the organization and target audience members.

The communication mode refers to the vehicle through which the message is received by the audience. For example, if a manager calls a customer on the telephone, the communication mode is the telephone. Communication modes can be either active or passive. An active communication mode refers to the case in which the message is pushed/sent by the organization (message sender) to the audience member (message receiver). A passive mode refers to the case in which the message is not received unless the audience member takes an action to acquire the message. Information that is placed on a website, for example, is an example of a passive message. The audience member must take an action (Google search, clicking on a link) to acquire the information. Examples of active communication modes or modalities are presented in Table 1.

Table 1. Active Modalities of Direct Organization-to-Audience Communication

Mode	Communication Quality
One-to-one, face-to-face conversation	Very good. Two-way and nonverbal communication facets are strong.
One-to-one, voice-to-voice conversation	Very good. Two-way and nonverbal facets are moderate.

One-to-one, text-to-text exchange	Fair. Two-way facet available, but weak. Nonverbal facet absent. Amount of information exchanged is restricted by mode.
One-to-many, in person-to-group	Moderate. Speaker can use nonverbal facet to improve communication directed at audience. Audience members can ask questions.
One-to-many, voice-to-voice (automated phone message, for example)	Weak. Two-way and nonverbal facets are absent. This mode may annoy audience.
One-to-many, message sent via post	Fair to moderate. Because this mode is more expense than using online methods, it is better received by the audience than in the past. This is especially true if the information is relevant to audience and informative rather than persuasive.
One to-many, message sent via email	Fair. Assuming double opt-in permission, this can be a good way to communicate with audience an informative, not persuasive, message.

In Table 1, some common examples of active modes of communication sent directly from the organization to audience members are provided. The quality of the communication is generally determined by two primary elements or facets: (1) whether or not the mode is two-way or one-way, and (2) whether or not the mode permits nonverbal communication. Two-way communicate means that those engaged in communication can be both senders and receivers of messages. Hence, audience members have an opportunity to ask clarifying questions to improve their understanding of the message. Managers have an opportunity to ask questions and receive responses from audience members to assess comprehension and to deliver more relevant examples and so forth.

With respect to the availability of nonverbal communications, it should be noted that only part of the communication between two people is derived from the words that are used. Eye contact, facial expression, body posturing, and tone of voice communicate a great deal about the emotional content of the communication and the level of understanding. The words are interpreted in the context of the nonverbal information. Depending on the situation, the nonverbal aspects of the communication can provide more information than the words that are used to express an idea.

There are many occasions when target audience members are receiving information about your brand object. An audience member's friend might talk about a recent experience with your brand (or one of its peers). Comments might be made about your brand on an independent website. An article in the local newspaper might discuss your brand. You might be able to have some influence on these externally generated messages or you might not.

1.2 Information you might influence, but cannot control

Often information that is disseminated about your organization may be outside of your sphere of influence. For example, the news media might report a story about your organization. An online blogger might offer opinions about your organization. At a public meeting, a citizen might make statements about your organization. In these examples, you want to be engaged in the conversations, where possible, in order to have some influence. If you do not get engaged, you will have no influence. The purpose of being engaged is to lessen any negative effects to your organization from externally generated information.

For example, imagine that you are the manager of a hotel chain. Because you have subscribed to Google Alerts or a media monitoring service, you have become aware of a guest complaint that was lodged on a popular site for tourist called TripAdviser. You can investigate the incident and respond appropriately to the guest and to the postings on TripAdviser. If you discover that the complaint is malicious or without a basis, you can lodge a complaint to TripAdvisor, which may remove the malicious posting. Even if the complaint is justified, a contrite posting of regret to the guest and a comment about identifying and correcting problems will make a favorable impression on TripAdviser visitors.

1.2.1 News media relations

News media relations refer to the relationships that an organization develops with journalists. Media refers to a communication channel used to communicate with large audiences. I distinguish between mass media and the news media. Mass media refers to any media (communication channel) that reaches a large audience. The news media refers to a type of mass media which has its content created by journalists (who aim to report on issues and matters of importance and relevance). Journalists have been trained in gathering, assessing, creating, and presenting news and information.

The news media is important to the organization because it presents information to the public about your organization that is perceived by audiences to be credible and objective. This includes information about issues related to your organization's purpose, mission, and operations. It is important for managers to be aware of information about the organization that is spread through the news media. Managers can respond to a story about the organization, retroactively (after the story has been published). Managers can attempt to influence the story proactively (before the story is published) by getting the organization's perspective presented to the journalist while the story is being developed. Having professional relationships with journalists helps because, although journalistic ethics prevents them from withholding an unpleasant truth about the organization, journalists will often allow the organization to present its own set of facts and perspectives while the story is being researched before it is published. Next I will present a series of steps to help build professional relationships with journalists.

The first step in news media relations is for managers to identify the news media sources that are most likely to cover stories about their organizations. Read and watch the news media in your local area. Subscribe to relevant newspapers and magazines; watch the local news; bookmark relevant news media websites; and join organizations in which you are likely to meet reporters and editors (some cities have press clubs you can join).

The second step in news media relations is to learn the names of the reporters who cover the topics most relevant to your organization. Do not forget about including specialized journalists who might be interested in your organization in special circumstances. If your organization is a local charity, for example, the calendar page editor will have an interest in your event listings. Most newspapers also carry a list of volunteer opportunities, so the charity can find out which person at the newspaper is responsible for this section.

The third step in news media relations is for managers to become better acquainted with the journalists they identified in Step 2. Start by arranging a short meeting at their newspaper headquarters or TV stations so you can introduce yourself. Be considerate of their busy schedules and make it brief. Drop off some printed material or personally deliver a press release instead of mailing or emailing it. Over time, you will have other opportunities to develop these contacts into more familiar relationships.

The fourth step in cultivating news media relationships is to regularly send complimentary copies of your publications to target journalists. Instead of just sending press copies to journalists along with your mass mailings, personally send a copy with your business card attached. You can also attach a note directing the reporter to some item in the publication that might be of particular interest. You can't just sign up journalists for your email communications (you need their permission first). But, once journalists are interested, they will likely subscribe to your email newsletter or follow your organization on social media. Do not forget to send journalists invitations to your special events. Even if they do not attend the events, the invitations will remind them of you and your organization. And be sure to work in as many informal contacts as possible with the journalists you are cultivating.

It is important to recognize that you goal is not to manipulate journalists. This would be unethical and you will fail in any event. Your goal for cultivating journalist relationships is twofold. First, you want journalists to have a sufficient level of understanding of your organization so that they will avoid errors when reporting stories involving your organization. Second, you want journalists to know how to contact you when they are researching a relevant story so that your perspective will be included in the journalists' research.

The fifth step in news media relations management is maintaining a current listing of journalists. Keep up with personnel changes at those news media organizations. The turnover in the media is often rapid. Develop your own media list and keep it up-to-date. You may be able to subscribe to a media list for your locality, but it can't substitute entirely for your own meticulously kept list. Look for reporters on social media and follow them there.

Step six is to be sure that the information you give to the news media is newsworthy. Your information should be new, noteworthy, and relevant to a large share of the public. Reporters are not interested in yesterday's news, items that are of interest only internally to your organization, or routine events. Provide reporters with good human interest stories. Invite staff and volunteers at your organization to let you know about good story ideas that you might be able to pitch to the media. The best ideas often come from people who are on the front lines of your organization.

Step seven—develop a virtual media kit that resides on your organization's website. When journalists are developing a story that has some connection with your organization, they may want to learn more about your organization. They may want to identify who in your organization to contact for an interview. The virtual media might include the history of your organization, its mission and goals, brief profiles and photos of key staff and board members, the most recent news releases, and a downloadable PDF of the current annual report. Busy journalists will appreciate being able to access this information easily.

Step eight—take advantage of breaking news stories to promote your organization. The best way to do this is to develop a cadre of "experts" who can speak to the issues your organization addresses. Train these experts in media interviewing techniques and make them available to reporters when there is a relevant news event. Colleges and universities often do this, taking advantage of the expertise among their faculty members. But even a small organization can get exposure in this way.

Step nine—make yourself available at any time. Always provide your email address on your press releases and on your website contact page. But also include a mobile number where journalists can reach you day or night. When you receive a call or a message from a journalist, get back to him or her as soon as you can. Journalists work on brief deadline schedules and will appreciate your prompt response.

Step ten—always thank journalists for their coverage. Initially, thank the reporter by email, but also follow up with a hand written thankyou note. Never underestimate the power of sincerely expressed appreciation. Plus, never complain about minor inaccuracies in a published story.

The information is already disseminated. Complaining about trivial inaccuracies is not worth your effort, and there is little to be gained by offending a busy journalist.

1.2.2 Communication management during a crisis

When an unexpected event, scandal, or crisis happens that involves your organization your organization may suddenly become the focal interest in a lot of news media coverage. The intensive and, perhaps, unfavorable coverage can have a marked influence on how various target audiences perceive your organization. For example, the Deepwater Horizon oil spill[3] effectively negated British Petroleum's (BP) prior investments in image advertising and social responsibility public relations efforts (deservedly so). BP's communications to the public and the news media during the oil spill appeared to have harmed the company more than helped it.[4]

The objective of organizational communications management is to lessen the negative impact on the organization from news coverage of the crisis. The magnitude of the BP oil spill was too great to allow BP to remain unaffected by the event. However, perhaps better management efforts could have lessened the negative effects.[5] Next, we will present six steps for crisis planning for more effective news media relations during times of crisis.

Step one—don't wait. Many organizations only get their crisis plans underway once a disaster has struck. Instead, brainstorm possible scenarios or types of disasters that could happen and start planning for them. Educate yourself about possible crises that might affect your type of

---

[3] See http://en.wikipedia.org/wiki/Deepwater_Horizon_oil_spill
[4] See http://www.cbsnews.com/news/bp-oil-spill-crisis-management-how-not-to-do-it/
[5] See http://www.cnn.com/2010/OPINION/06/21/kimberly.bp.management.crisis/

organization and talk to those organizations that experienced those crises. Invite a veteran of a crisis to speak to your staff and your board, discussing their experiences and what they learned. Assign relevant staff members to draft a crisis plan. Advocate for good crisis preparedness. Many managers, especially those leading small organizations, don't think anything bad will ever happen; they don't want to think about it; they don't think they have the time to prepare; and they might even resent staff members recommend planning for a crisis.

Step two—realize that crises take many forms. Crises come in all varieties. Some will attract a great deal of media attention while others might be largely overlooked. But, in a time of the internet and cable television news, thinking you can keep the situation out of the public eye is a fantasy. The various media outlets will require different responses. Prepare for as many as you can imagine, and do your best to put plans into place that will minimize the damage to your organization's reputation.

Even if something happens that you didn't anticipate, your preparation for other types of emergencies will help. Practicing any emergency response is likely to make your organization better prepared for others.

Step three—develop a communications plan. A communications plan involves identifying spokespeople, assigning someone to gather the facts as they emerge, writing press releases, setting up a media hotline (a telephone number that will connect journalists directly to the relevant organization member), and finding a venue where you can conduct a press conference. These activities can be arranged in advance.

Step four—develop your social media capabilities in advance. Social media can be a blessing during a crisis if it is effectively managed. Most organizations now use social media. Decide in advance who will manage social media during a crisis situation. Set up a dashboard[6] where social media channels can be monitored and responses provided quickly.

Because of the nature of social media, there is little ability to control information. But you can, through monitoring and offering prompt and useful responses, provide good information, fight rumors with fact, and express concern. Social media may well be the best way to show the human face of your organization and shore up its reputation for being kind, sympathetic, polite, accurate, and a source of unbiased information.

Step five—be prepared to communicate. Every minute counts after a crisis. Don't waste time. Deliver appropriate statements and messages immediately, even if it is to only say that you know about the situation, you're working on it, and that few facts are known at the moment. Then maintain communications with updates as the facts become better understood.

In all communications be concerned, show sincerity, speak clearly, and always tell the truth. Don't be afraid to say, "We don't know." That is better than guessing. Add that you are working as quickly as possible to get all the facts. Far more is lost by refusing to speak to the media than is risked by doing so. A vacuum of information breeds media hostility and public loss of confidence.

Step six—make sure relevant people in your organization are trained to work with news media. Put together a media training program before disaster strikes. Train anyone who might need to be a spokesperson. That would be your key board members, your CEO and other key staff. Think broadly when deciding who to train. Media training needn't cost much if you have someone on your board who works in public relations or someone who is a member of the media. The key point is to ensure that key

---

[6] See http://www.klipfolio.com/resources/dashboard-examples/social-media

staff members are trained to work with the news media.

- Make sure that key staff members are trained to work with the news media.

Brand strength is determined by the perceptions of your target audiences. Their perceptions are formed from the information they receive from all sources, as well as their personal experiences with your organization, its products, or its services. Your organization can control the information it distributes. Sometimes, your organization can influence information that is spread apart from the organization. However, it is not always possible to influence externally generated information about your organization.

1.3 Information you cannot control

A great deal of the information transmitted about your organization is beyond your control. People are generally free to say what they please. When what they say about your organization in unfavorable or inaccurate, your ability to react to this information is limited. The purpose of the prior section (news media relations and crises communications) was to show you how you can have greater influence over externally generated information.

At this point in our discussion, it is time to emphasize an important concept.

- The more familiar target audiences are with your organization, the less likely they will be to accept information that is inconsistent with their beliefs about your organization.

For example, let's assume your best friends (presumably individuals who know you very well) hear a vicious rumor regarding your personal conduct. Your best friends know you very well. They have formed an enduring comprehension of the type of person you are and what is typical of your normal behavior. When confronted with the malicious rumor, they will view this alleged misconduct as being beyond the bounds of what is normal behavior for you. They will, therefore, reject the rumor as false gossip.

Similarly, when target audiences know an organization very well, they have formed an enduring comprehension of the organization. When that comprehension of the organization is very positive, they are unlikely to believe false accusations that they believe are outside of the boundaries of what would be considered your organization's normal conduct.

- A high level of brand strength provides some degree of inoculation against harmful accusations against your organization.

When your best friends believe you to have a high level of personal integrity, they will be skeptical when receiving information that you have behaved in a dishonorable manner. Additionally, if you challenge the rumor and confront the person making the allegation, your indignation will be viewed as credible and received as further evidence of your innocence.

When target audiences of an organization with high brand strength receive slanderous information about your organization that is contrary to their comprehension of your brand, they will likewise be skeptical. Your organization's challenge to the source of the information will be viewed as credible and further evidence of the rumor's falsehood.

- When brand strength is high, the harm of false allegations can be deflected.

When the rumor of misconduct is proven true, however, this can have a damaging effect on brand strength. The amount of damage is dependent upon the nature and severity of the misconduct. Misconduct that is comparatively minor and limited to an organizational member of minor importance may be viewed as an anomaly and not a manifestation of a systemic organizational problem. Misconduct that is major, long-term, and performed by the leadership team may be viewed as the more truthful nature of the organization and might replace the earlier comprehension audiences had of the organization. Imagine for example that one of your best friends committed a series of terrible acts that you only recently discovered. You might reasonably conclude that you really did not know that person (original comprehension was false) and that the *real* person (the more valid comprehension of the person) is quite unfavorable.

The damage of truthful allegations of misconduct can be even greater if the organization initially denies or challenges the allegations. When an organization claims that truthful allegations of misconduct are false, and when the organization challenges the motives of the person making the allegations, the damage to the organization can be greater when the truth of the allegations is proven. This is because the denials of misconduct, interpreted in the context of allegations proven to be true, are perceived to be (1) confirmation of the misconduct as evidence of the true nature of the organization, (2) evidence that the organization does not regret its misconduct, and (3) evidence that the organization is deceptive and cannot be trusted. The lesson to be learned from these concepts is to make sure your conduct is beyond reproach.

1.4 Personal experiences with brand

While the information target audience members receive about the brand object helps them to form an understanding of the brand, their personal experiences with the brand object are also important. Personal experiences with the brand object carry the greatest weight in forming an understanding of the brand. Personal experiences with the brand's peers help the target audience develop standards of comparisons for the peer brand class.

Managers need to appreciate the importance of ensuring that target audience experiences with the organization, its products and services, are consistently excellent. Unfortunately, managers sometimes give too little attention to the quality of the personal interactions between organization personnel and target audience members.

- Managers need to make sure that target audience experiences with the brand object and the organization are always positive experiences.

2.0 Strategic and tactical messaging

An important concept presented in this book is that building brand strength is a long-term endeavor. Each year, an organization should aim to increase its brand strength. Over a span of years, if the annually-implemented brand strength tactics have been successful, the brand will become stronger. Harvard University did not become a prestigious university right away. It began with only nine students in 1636.[7] Today, Harvard is one of the most prestigious universities in the world.

There are two important points to note:

- Becoming a strong, dominant brand requires years of incremental annual increases in brand strength.

---

[7] See http://www.harvard.edu/history

- The time required to become a strong, dominant brand is influenced by the degree to which the brand object is remarkable. The more remarkable the brand object, the less time required to become a strong, dominant brand.

At this point, I would like to distinguish between strategic communications and tactical communications. Strategic communications are developed to attain long-term goals that pertain to the entire organization. For example, in the previous chapter, we used a fictitious hotel chain to illustrate brand remarkability planning. We will use the hotel chain for our communications example here. Our strategic communications will be planned and implemented for the purpose of achieving our strategic goal. Our strategic goal is for our hotel chain to become the strongest brand (dominant brand) in its class within five years. The hotel class refers to the target audience whose patronage (support) our hotel and its peers compete to attract. In our hotel example, the target audience is vacationing families on a budget.

Simply having a strategic goal is insufficient to guide the planning of strategic communications. We need to understand the organization's plan for achieving its goal. For our hotel chain, we believe we can become the dominant brand by offering our target audience the best value. We are not the least expensive hotel. However, for a modest increase in price, compared to similar hotels, our guests get much higher quality and better services than offered by our peer brands (competitors). We believe our target audience will be willing to pay a little more than the lowest rate available in order to have a superior guest experience.

Over the five-year period we have given ourselves to achieve our strategic goal, we will have to incrementally increase brand remarkability in order to achieve our desired positioning with respect to our peer brands. The examples in the prior chapter discussed this process at length. During the five-year period, we will have annual communication plans in which we will communicate our positioning message. We will promote the superior value and quality service our guests will experience by choosing us. Referring to the peer brands (Hotel A and Hotel B) used in the prior chapter, our messages will explain to our target audiences that:

- Although Hotel A is cheaper, our hotel offers a great deal more benefits and higher quality for a marginally higher rate—making it a great value.
- Hotel B is more expensive than our hotel. Our hotel offers better quality that Hotel B. Therefore, our hotel is a better value.

Communicating our remarkability to our target audiences will increase our brand strength. Increasing our brand strength annually over a sufficiently long period of time will eventually result in our brand becoming the dominant brand (the strongest brand in its class).

The prolonged emphasis on building brand strength is an example of strategic communications. Organizations will have other goals they want to attain in the near term. A store, for example, may want to have an off-season sale to reduce inventory and increase short-term revenue. A charity may want to implement a volunteer recruitment campaign. A city may want to have an arts festival to promote arts and culture in its community. Communications that are implemented to achieve short-term goals not related to strategic objectives are examples of tactical communications. Tactical communications refers to messages disseminated to our target audiences for the purpose of attaining short-term (typically one-year or less) goals.

Organizations' annual communication plans will contain portions that are intended to further their strategic goals. They will also contain portions that are intended to achieve short-term tactical goals. Communication plans, then, contain campaigns that are intended to achieve short-term goals and to help achieve long-term goals. Communication plans are a mixture of campaigns designed to achieve both tactical and strategic goals.

3.0 Developing the annual communication plan

We will now discuss the components contained in a typical annual communication plan. Remember that the purpose of the communication plan is to achieve the desired objectives for which has been created. The communication plan is an ends to a means. Remember that the best plan is of little value if it is not implemented effectively. Also be mindful of the reality that the organization has to provide the resources necessary to implement the plan.

3.1 Step 1 – Define your objectives

Because the communication plan is designed to achieve the objectives for which it has been created, the manner in which the objectives are stated is quite important. If the objectives are not stated clearly and precisely, it will be more difficult to develop a successful communication plan.

The objectives should be stated in a manner that leads to their measurement. You must be able to determine whether or not, and by how much, an objective has been achieved. Hence, objectives must be stated in terms of variables (what is to be measured?), quantity (what level of the variable is considered necessary to achieve the goal?), and timing (when is the goal's attainment desired?).

- Properly stated goals and objectives should answer the what, how much, and when questions.

The objectives should reflect a continuous improvement management orientation. Successful brand management requires continually improving brand remarkability. An emphasis on continually improving brand remarkability is consistent with good management practices which should emphasize continually improving the organization.

Some examples of marketing objectives that are measurable and reflect a continuous improvement orientation are:

- We will increase brand strength 10% by the end of this year.
- We will increase our audience brand recall from 4th position to 2nd position by the end of this year.
- We will increase brand familiarity by 15% by the end of this year.
- We will increase our donor retention rate from 40% to 45% by year's end.
- We will reduce our customer defection rate by 10% the end of this year.
- We want to attract 10,000 attendees at this year's heritage festival.
- We would like to sell 1,500 season tickets for this year's community theatre productions.
- We want to add $2 million our university endowment by year's end.
- We want our political party to increase it favorability rating by 20% with the target audience represented by working class young adults, ages 18 to 25, by election day.

Note that examples of goals are provided for different types of organizations. Each goal is stated in terms of variables like brand strength, brand recall, brand familiarity, donor retention, and so forth. Each goal specifies the desired change in the respective variable. The variable change reflects improvements over the current status (continuous improvement orientation). Note that in a couple of examples (season tickets, festival attendance), the deadline is implicit.

It may be the case that an organization has not previously measured a specific variable, but the organization wants to see improvement in that area. For example, prior to reading this book, a manager might never have measured brand strength. After learning about the strategic importance of brand strength, however, the manager realizes that increasing brand strength is quite important. In this case, the goal should state by how much the previously-unmeasured variable is expected to increase over the year. The first example above states that brand strength should increase by 10% by year's end. The organization can measure brand strength at the beginning of the year and at the end of the year. As another option, the manager could establish the goal of measuring brand strength (for the first time) to establish a baseline for planning future projected growth in brand strength.

New variables for which the organization lacks a history of measurement are more difficult to predict in goal-setting. It will be difficult to determine what tactics will result in a 10 percent brand strength increase if brand strength has not been previously measured. However, if the organization had several years of setting goals and implementing plans to achieve those goals for increases in brand strength, desired improvements could be more realistic and precise, and the plans developed to achieve those goals could be more effective. Over time, with experience and experimentation, managers will learn what they can accomplish with much greater accuracy.

3.2 Step 2 – Determine your core message

Your core message is the argument or claim you will present in your messages that depict your brand remarkability. In our hotel chain example, our core message is that our hotel offers the best value. Compared to Hotel A, our guests get a much better experience (higher quality and more amenities) for a marginally higher price. Compared to Hotel B, our guests get the same or better quality experience for a lower price.

The core message may not be a central part of every communication campaign. It will, however, be a key component of the majority of your messaging in order to achieve your strategic goals. The core message will be a key aspect of a campaign for increasing brand strength.

Another important benefit of understanding your core message is that it provides a consistent theme across the various campaigns. The core message lets managers know what brand attributes should be emphasized in messages. Without this consistency, when there are different brand attributes being emphasized in different campaigns, the brand meaning loses focus. The target audience is directed towards different brand attributes, some of which are not indicators of brand remarkability. Brand strength is lowered as a result.

3.3 Step 3 – Profile your audiences

The better you understand your target audiences, the better informed you will be in deciding how best to communicate with them. A superficial profile of your audiences tells you little about how to reach them with your messages and what communication channels are most effective. If your target audience is made of young highly-educated unmarried women, you would use different communication pathways and different words and images than if your target audience is made of middle-age, working-class, married men.

Some variables that can be used to profile an audience helps you identify them. The more completely you can identify your target audience, the more likely you will be to select the appropriate communication channels. As an example, imagine that you own a restaurant in your community. A naïve manager might argue that anyone in the community is part of the target audience. Everyone eats, after all. Anyone in the community could, potentially, eat in the community restaurant. While these points are factually true, they tell us little about which target audiences in the community are most likely to find the restaurant an appealing place to eat. What features distinguish the restaurant? Is it an expensive restaurant? Is it an inexpensive restaurant? What kind of food does it feature? What is the general quality of the food? How long does the average group stay while dining? Does the restaurant offer alcoholic beverages? It is likely that the restaurant has brand attributes which make it more attractive to some people than to other people.

One way to profile an audience is by using demographic variables that distinguish target audience members from the general population. Demographic variables are personal statistics that might include information like income level, gender, education level, age, marital status, ethnicity, family size and composition, home ownership status, or geographic location.

To enrich the target audience profile, psychographic variables might also be useful. Psychographics refers to lifestyle characteristics. Psychographic variables include people's activities, interests, and opinions. What club memberships are common among target audience members? Do target audience members share any core values, opinions, hobbies, or interests? Are there any similar recreational activities that are favored? Are there similarities among target audience members with respect to religious beliefs or religious service attendance? What types of music, television, or entertainment is preferred by the target audience?

As the profile of your target audience becomes more refined, you will have better information to help you select the most effective communication channels for delivering your messages to your target audience. You will also have better information to help you develop the most persuasive messages for your target audiences.

3.4 Step 4 – Identify communication channels or pathways

A rich understanding of your target audiences will help you identify the most effective pathways or channels for delivering your messages. Many media outlets (radio, television, newspapers, and magazines) hire audience research firms like Nielsen to conduct audience surveys[8] to match media outlets with audience sizes and profiles. Media outlets should be able to describe to a potential advertiser their audience's demographic profile and size.

Managers can identify media outlets (communication channels) that attract audiences that are similar to their own target audiences. A communication channel refers to the medium or vehicle through which a message is sent to its target audience, such as print media (newspapers, magazines) or broadcast media (television, radio).

3.4.1 Types of communication channels

There are various ways to classify communication channels. There are also a large variety of different communication channels. Hence, we will necessarily avoid attempting to describe every way to classify communication channels or listing every example of a communication channel.

One way to classify communication channels is offline versus online

---

[8] See http://en.wikipedia.org/wiki/Audience_measurement

channels. The key distinction is that online communication channels use either the internet or mobile telephone networks to transmit information. The average person is exposed to over 3,000 marketing messages daily.[9] To attract attention amid all this information clutter, clever marketers continue to find new ways of reaching audiences. Table 2 lists some examples of offline communication channels. Table 3 lists some examples of online communication channels. There are several channels in each category. Choose the combination that makes sense for your resources and objectives. Offline and online channels should complement each other and should have an integrated message.

Table 2. Offline Channel Examples

Television – broadcast/cable	Mail/post	Posters
Radio	Billboard	Street advertising
Newspaper	Kiosks	Promotional products
Magazines & periodicals	Bus advertising	Aerial advertising

Table 3. Online Channel Examples[10]

Web banner advertising	Email	Mobile advertising
Search engine advertising	e-newsletters	Affiliate marketing
Social networks	Action alerts	Adware
Social media	E-zines	Content marketing

Effective communication requires exposing your audience to your message a sufficient number of times so that the audience remembers your message. Repeating your message a few times is a good way to accomplish this. However, after four or five exposures, audience members begin to avoid giving additional repeated messages their attention. Hence, it is a good practice to combine repetition with redundancy.

---

[9] See http://www.quora.com/How-many-marketing-messages-are-we-exposed-to-daily

[10] See http://en.wikipedia.org/wiki/Online_advertising

Redundancy refers to sending your message to your audience using a different method (copy and artwork) and different channel. Copy refers to the word choice used to communicate your message. Artwork refers to the nonverbal elements of your message. Find a couple of different ways to present your message to your audience. Developing different advertisements and sending them through different media outlets is a good way to develop a communications mix that will maintain your audience's attention. Obviously, it is important to select channels that will be effective in communicating your message.

- It is useful to present your message to your audiences multiple times.
- Repetition is helpful to establish enduring memories; but after a point, repetition's effectiveness diminishes.
- Redundancy is presenting the message in a different way so that it doesn't feel like the exact same message (repetition) to the receiver.
- Typically, it will take the audience at least six exposures to your redundantly-delivered messaged to establish a memory for that message.

3.4.2 Channel effectiveness

In general, communication effectiveness improves the closer a channel is to representing face-to-face communication between two people who are members of the same social network. Figure 1 illustrates this principle. Remember that this is a general rule. There are exceptions.

The implication of Figure 1 is that managers should use interpersonal communication channels, if practical. For example, pharmaceutical companies invest heavily in teams of sales representatives that visit physicians[11] in order to use face-to-face communication. The sales representatives sometimes will buy lunch for the entire office staff (the office clinic will be closed to patients during lunch) in order to have a captive audience to discuss a company's branded drug. For another example, political candidates running for an elected office often speak to people one-on-one. Candidates also recruit volunteers who canvas neighborhoods in order to talk individually to potential voters.

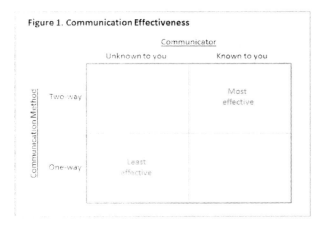

Figure 1. Communication Effectiveness

It is not always practical to interact individually with members of a target audience. There may be a large number of people in your target audience. The audience may be geographically dispersed. In this case, appropriate communication channels should be selected that will effectively reach your target audience.

When selecting a communication channel, reach and frequency are important considerations. Reach refers to the proportion of an organization's

---

[11] See https://www.youtube.com/watch?v=jhV0zDVXd18

target audience that will receive the message if transmitted through a particular communication channel. A communication channel that reaches only a tiny fraction of your target audience is probably best avoided.

Frequency refers to the number of times your target audience members will receive your message. Frequency is achieved through message repetition and by rotating advertisements (redundancy) between different communication channels. Managers should plan for a frequency of about six. That is, audience members should be exposed to the message about six times *as a minimum*. It would be better to expose audience members to a redundant message through different communication pathways between six and 12 times during the year.

- Try to expose target audience members to your message between six and 12 times.

- Communicate your central message using different message formats (different copy and artwork) and different communication pathways.

3.5 Step 5 – Establish your time table

There are two essential steps in establishing your time table. First, you need to develop your media scheduling plan. Then, you need to establish a composite time table that includes a means of accountability. The communication plan will likely have multiple objectives, requiring multiple campaigns. The multiple campaigns will be combined into a composite communications plan.

3.5.1 Message scheduling

A decision that needs to be made with respect to communication channels is message scheduling. Message scheduling refers to planning the time
period and intensity of target audience message exposure. The best message phasing schedule is dependent upon the nature of the campaign being
implemented by the organization. Some considerations are:

- How often should your audience be exposed to your message?
  - (Frequency)
- How many times during the year should you present your message
  to your audience?
  - (Number of exposures)
- How should the delivery of your messages be timed or spaced dur-
  ing your planning period?

Figure 2 shows an example of evenly spaced message phasing, called
continuous scheduling. In this example, a message is delivered to your target audience at regular intervals. Continuous scheduling is useful to remind
the audience of your brand remarkability. As audience memory fades or de-
cays, the next media cycle serves to remind and refresh the message in the
minds of audience members (strengthening the memory for better accessibility and retention).

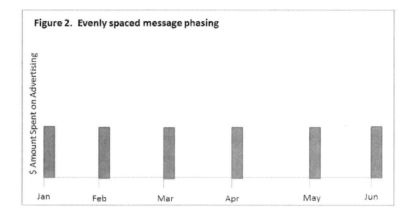

Figure 3 shows an example of irregularly spaced message scheduling, called flighting. In this message scheduling plan, messages are presented to the audience intensively for irregular periods of time. For examples, many retail stores advertise most heavily during the Christmas shopping season. Since about half of their sales may occur during this period, it makes sense to communicate to audiences when they are doing much of their shopping. Stores may also have periodic seasonal sales, which require advertising support during those periods.

One advantage of flighting is that advertisers can buy more message space than competitors during a short period of time. Keep in mind that the most effective campaign will present audience members with a series of different advertisements, having a consistent message, and delivered using different media vehicles.

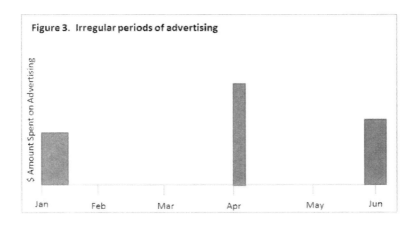

Figure 4 shows pulsed media scheduling. Pulsing combines both continuous scheduling and flighting. It combines a low frequency of regularly spaced year-round advertising with heavy (high frequency) advertising during specific periods. Pulsing combines the advantages of continuous and flighting scheduling. That is, the continuous component of the flighting scheduling plan might deliver messages aimed at building brand strength. The pulsing component of the flighting scheduling plan might deliver messages aimed at attaining short-term objectives (sales, promotions, event attendance).

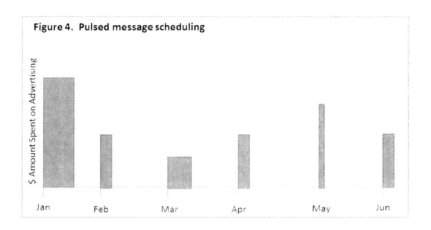

Figure 4. Pulsed message scheduling

3.5.2 Constructing a composite time table with accountability

Each campaign is developed to achieve a specified objective that was identified in Step 1. In a sense, then, managers specify their objectives in Step 1. In the remaining steps, the campaigns are developed that, when implemented effectively, should attain their respective goals.

Each campaign will involve a series of tactics that need to be implemented at the desired time. A campaign calendar should be created which shows when each tactic is to be implemented. The person who is responsible for making sure that a campaign tactic is successfully implemented should be identified in the campaign's narrative or description or on the campaign event calendar. Having someone assigned to a campaign tactic provides some degree of accountability to the extent that someone is responsible for overseeing the implementation of the tactic.

Depending on the complexity of your plan, this can be a spreadsheet that shows when various elements of your communications program are activated. You might have to develop a general spreadsheet for the entire program, and then worksheets to provide specifics for individual campaigns. You will need to provide sufficient detail in describing your plan so that your organization understands it easily (including identifying who will implement each part of the plan).

Recall that each goal usually requires its own campaign (set of tactics needed for its attainment). An organization's communication *plan* contains the various campaigns. The scheduling calendar will reflect this relationship. Each campaign will have its relevant schedule. The various campaign schedules will be combined into a composite schedule for the entire communication plan.

3.5.3 Charity example

As an example to illustrate some of the concepts I have discussed, I will use a simple example of a fictitious charity (see Figure 5). In this example, the organization has identified six communication objectives or goals (see Step 1) that it wants to attain in the following year. Notice that a campaign has been developed to achieve each goal. The implementation of each campaign will require the completion of a series of tasks.

Figure 5. Charity example

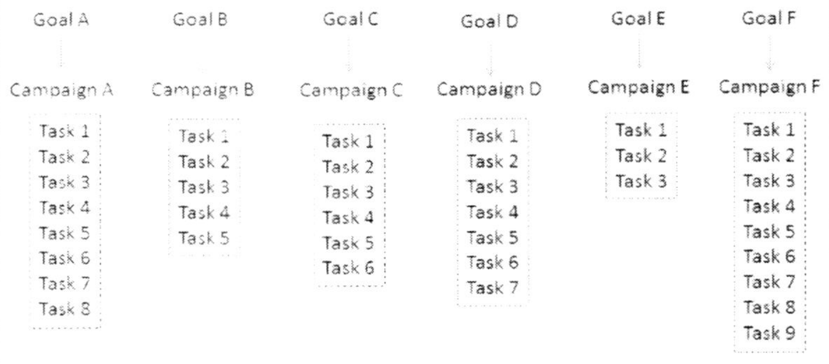

In Figure 6, I illustrate that the communication plan for the organization is a combination of the various campaigns that are depicted in Figure 5. Although this is a simple point, it is often a point of confusion. Hence, we want to make a special effort to clarify the relationship between the organization's communication plan which is made from a combination of the various campaigns.

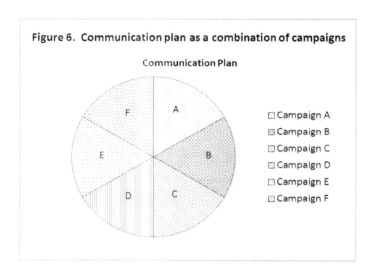

Figure 6. Communication plan as a combination of campaigns

Communication Plan

☐ Campaign A
▨ Campaign B
☐ Campaign C
▥ Campaign D
☐ Campaign E
▨ Campaign F

To further elaborate our charitable example, let us specify Goal C (for which Campaign C will be created). Goal C for our charity is created to address the charity's need to recruit 50 new volunteers by March 1st. We have determined that there are three sources from which we will recruit our volunteers: internal sources, advertising, and our city's volunteer center.

The tasks that need to be implemented in Campaign C in order to attain Goal C are listed in Table 4.

Once the relevant campaign tasks have been identified that are needed to attain the goal, it is time to develop a timeline for performing the various tasks. In our example, we need the 50 new volunteers by March 1st. It makes sense, in our situation, to work from March 1st, backwards.

Table 4. Campaign C Tasks

Recruitment source	Tasks
All	Update and revise existing volunteer job descriptions
Internal	Develop recruitment prospect lists • Referrals from staff • Referrals from current volunteers • Referrals from board members • Donor lists Develop recruitment message Deliver appeal to prospects
Advertising	Create newspaper ad Schedule ad to appear in newspaper
Local volunteer center	Contact local volunteer center
All	Screening of applicants • Review completed applications • Check references • Conduct background checks Training of new recruits • Schedule site tours • Schedule classroom training • Schedule on-the-job training Orientation • Match new recruit with mentor • Introduce new recruit to other volunteers, staff, and leadership

In Table 5, we present the timing of the various tasks, showing when they will have to be performed in order to attain our goal of recruiting 50 new volunteers. Note that an individual has been assigned responsibility for overseeing each task.

Table 5. Campaign C Time Line

Timing	Event	Person
March 1st	50 new volunteers ready to serve	
Feb 15-25	On-the-job training	Jessica
Feb 1-1	Orientation	Bob
Jan 15-30	On site tours and classroom training	Jessica
Dec 1 to Jan 10	Screen of applicants	Sarah
Nov 1 to Dec 15	Newspaper ads are published	Judy
Nov 1 to Dec 15	Internally generated prospect list is contacted	Bob
Nov 1-15	Contact local volunteer center	Judy
Oct 1-31	Develop prospect list from internal sources	Bob

In practice, these example tables would be part of a report which describes in greater detail all aspects of the campaign. Each task would contain sufficient detail so that the task is easily understood and implemented without any significant additional planning. When done this way, the organization's marketing team can meet periodically to discuss progress on the various campaigns and to determine what corrections or changes need to be made.

3.6 Step 6 – Develop prototypes

A prototype refers to a preliminary model of a communication element that will be used in a campaign. Communication elements refer to the various formatted messages that will be used. These might include a storyboard for a television ad, a newspaper ad, a radio script, a brochure, a poster, a diagram of a website, and so forth. The prototypes are included in the communication plan in order to illustrate the nature of the communication element that will ultimately be used in a campaign.

For example, if a campaign will use a television commercial, a prototype might be in the form of a four panel storyboard that shows the basic features and script of the scenes in the commercial. A storyboard is composed of a sequence of drawings, typically with some directions and dialogue, representing the various scenes used in a television commercial.

A radio commercial's prototype might be the script that will later be produced into a 30 or 60 second radio announcement or ad. Sketches of web pages, posters, billboards, or brochures can also serve as useful prototypes. The prototype for a direct mail packet might include an example cover letter, outer envelope, and any inserts that might be included.

3.7 Step 7 – Establish a means of evaluation

In Step 1, we discussed defining our objectives for the communication plan. We described the outcomes we wanted to achieve during the year. The campaigns comprising the communication plan were developed to achieve their respective objectives. One requirement for our objectives was that they are measureable. If an objective is not stated in terms that can be measured, then it is impossible to determine the degree to which we have attained that objective.

In Step 7, we describe how the variables identified in our Step 1 objectives will be measured. If the variable (sales, for example) is currently measured on a regular basis, then we can specify that we will measure the variable using our ongoing method of measurement for that variable. Other variables might not be currently measured by your organization, and would require a means of measurement.

Most organizations have developed ways to measure accounting variables, which use money as the unit of measurement. Accounting variables are concerned about keeping track of cash inflows and outflows (accounts receivable and debts are postponed cash inflows and outflows). Accounting systems count an organization's money in categories of assets, liabilities, revenues, and expenses.

While marketing managers are interested in some of the variables typically measured in accounting systems, there are variables of interest to marketing professionals for which accountants may not share an interest. For example, marketing professionals are keenly interested in customer acquisition and retention. They are interested in brand strength. They are interested customer satisfaction.

If an organization conducts a regular survey from samples of its target audiences, then a new variable might be measured as part of the survey. For example, brand strength can be measured using a series of nine questions in a survey. For Step 7 of the communication plan, you would want to list the nine questions that will be used to measure brand strength, and indicate that these questions will be added to the annual survey conducted by the organization.

If the organization does not conduct periodic audience surveys, then you will have to describe details for conducting your own survey (assuming a survey is the method you will need to measure your variable). In this case, you will have to describe how many completed surveys you will need, your anticipated response rate, your sample size, where you will obtain your sample frame (a listing of target audience contact information), and the questions you will include in your survey.

Some variables will be measured using other techniques. For example, if you own a store and you are interested in measuring monthly customer visits, you can put a device on the door that counts each time the door is opened. If you wanted to measure customer retention, you could create accounts (telephone numbers, email addresses, loyalty card numbers) and monitor the account activity.

For Step 7, you should list which variables will be measured to assess your level of attaining the various Step 1 objectives. Then you should describe how each variable will be measured, including as much detail as possible.

3.8 Step 8 – Develop your budget

The implementation of your communication plan will require funding. Therefore, you will need to develop a budget for your plan's implementation. Each campaign will have its own budget. Then you will combine the various campaign budgets into an overall budget for the communication plan (see Chapter 5). Hence, you will be able to assess the cost of attaining each objective. You will be able to determine the total funding you will need as well and the required funding on a monthly basis.

3.8.1 Campaign budgets

Each campaign activity that will require funding should be included in your campaign budget. The cost estimates should be as precise as possible. For example, let us imagine that one campaign of a communication plan (Campaign A) will require a direct mail campaign, and a series of radio ads. The direct mail portion of the campaign will be implemented in March. The radio ad portion of the campaign will be implemented in October. An example budget for Campaign A is presented in Table 6.

It is important that the estimates be accurate. The cost estimate for the brochure creative work (based on our prototype) was generated from a graphic artist. The direct mail printing estimates were acquired (using our prototypes) by contacting three different printers (so we could find a competitive price). The cost for acquiring the addresses we will need for our direct mail was acquired by contacting a list broker.[12] We acquired the postage rates from the postal service's website.

---

[12] See http://en.wikipedia.org/wiki/List_broker

Table 6. Campaign A Budget

Expense item	Estimate	Component/Timing
Creative work – brochure	$300	Direct mail - March
Printing 5,000 direct mail packets (includes outer envelope, cover letter, brochure, & coupon insert)	$5,000	Direct mail – March
Acquiring 5,000 addresses	$250	Direct mail – March
Postage	$1,250	Direct mail – March
Sub-total (direct mail)	**$6,800**	
Production of radio ad	$200	Radio ads - October
30 ads (drive time)	$4,500	Radio ads - October
Sub-total (radio)	**$4,700**	
Total (Campaign A)	**$11,500**	

From our audience profile, we know which radio station we will use to reach our target audience. The radio station's website had an advertising rate card, from which we were able to get the cost of purchasing 30 60-second radio ads during drive time.[13] We had to call the radio station and talk to an account representative to find out how much it would cost ($200) to hire one of the radio station's on air hosts to read and record the script (from our prototype) to use in the 60-second ads.

3.8.2 Communication plan budget

When all the budgets for the separate campaigns are developed, an overall grand budget for the communication plan can be created. A simple communication plan budget is presented in Table 7.

---

[13] See http://en.wikipedia.org/wiki/Drive_time

Camp	Jan	Feb	Mar	Apr	May	Jun	Jul	Aug	Sep	Oct	Nov	Dec	Total
A			6,800							4,700			11,500
B	500	500	500	500	500	500	500	500	500	500	500	500	6,000
C	1,250	800			750		3,000						5,800
D			1,500	1,500	1,500							8,000	12,500
Total	1,750	1,300	8,800	2,000	2,750	500	3,500	500	500	5,200	500	8,500	35,800

Table 7. Communication plan budget

Note that the expense for Campaign A (from Table 6) is contained in the communication plan budget presented in Table 7. The direct mail component of Campaign A will incur expenses in March ($6,800). The radio ad component of Campaign A will incur expenses in October ($4,700). The simple example plan in Table 7 contains four campaigns (A through D). Creating a table for the communication plan budget allows you to see the cost for each campaign, the costs for all campaigns, and the expenses that will be incurred on a monthly basis. Hence, the accounting/finance professionals in your organization can make sure that sufficient funding is available when needed.

3.8.3 Budget negotiating process

The process described here begins with the goals that the organization wants to attain, then the activities that are required to attain those goals are developed, and then the costs of implementing those activities are estimated. This process is presented in Figure 7.

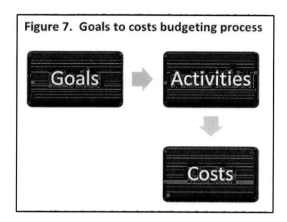

Figure 7. Goals to costs budgeting process

This is the recommend process to follow. It is a rational process. The costs of funding a communication plan are derived from the activities required to attain the desired goals. The goals are established in Step 1 in developing our annual communication plan. Steps 2 through 6 involve the development of activities that are needed to attain the goals. In Step 7, the costs of implementing those activities are estimated.

If your organization's leadership believes the costs are too great, then you can collaborate in order to identify (1) areas in which cost estimates are erroneously high or (2) activities that are not needed to attain their intended outcome goal. If either of these two conditions is not met and your organization's executive still believes the costs are too great, then the only reasonable action to take to reduce the size of the budget is to remove a goal and its accompanying campaign. This action requires your organization's executive to rank the goals with respect to their importance (priority) to the organization. The least important goal/campaign is deleted first, and so on, until the executive is satisfied with the communication plan expense totals.

CPSIA information can be obtained
at www.ICGtesting.com
Printed in the USA
LVOW10s1935121117
556011LV00011B/655/P